A Separate Development

Christopher Hope

A Separate Development

ROUTLEDGE & KEGAN PAUL
London and Henley

First published in Great Britain in 1981
by Routledge & Kegan Paul Ltd
39 Store Street, London WC1E 7DD and
Broadway House, Newtown Road,
Henley-on-Thames, Oxon RG9 1EN

Set in IBM 10 on 12pt Century by
Columns, Reading
and printed in Great Britain by
St Edmundsbury Press, Bury St Edmunds, Suffolk

British Library Cataloguing in Publication Data

Hope, Christopher

A separate development.
I. Title
823[F]   PR9369.2.H/

ISBN 0-7100-0954-2

"... Yes, my eyes are closed to your light. I am a beast, a Negro. But I can be saved. You are false negroes, you maniacs, savages, misers. Merchant, you are a negro; magistrate, you are a negro; general, you are a negro; emperor, old tease, you are a negro; you have drunk an untaxed liquor from Satan's distillery. — This is a people inspired by fever and cancer. The crippled and the old are so respectable that they ought to be boiled. The most artful course is to leave this continent where lunacy roams to supply hostages to these wretches. I am entering the true kingdom of the children of Ham."

Rimbaud *A Season in Hell*

"The trouble with Gawie Erasmus," Koos said, "is that he is not really a white man. It doesn't show in his hair or his finger-nails, of course. He is not as coloured as all that. But you can tell it easily in other ways. Yes, that is what's wrong with Gawie. His Hottentot forbears."

Herman Charles Bosman *Marico Scandal*

1

Let's say it began that afternoon when I exposed myself to
Mina Meintjies. That's how she will remember it, I'm sure.
I was standing on the edge of Jack Wyner's swimming pool,
that shapely blue kidney, under a hot sun, near the steps at
the shallow end, balanced carefully on the curved lip which
jutted a couple of inches over the water. Mina was looking
up . . .

I think about where it all began because I have to do so. It is
a question I am often asked and one I often ask myself — for
reasons which will become clear, and possibly rather painful,
as this statement of *fact* — I emphasise fact, for that is what
it is — gets under way. I might add that I don't wish to
remember where it all began. I would prefer to forget.
However, this is not allowed. If I am to have any hope of
freedom, everything must come out. The theory seems to be
that as long as it all comes out, a pattern will emerge which
will enable others to work out just what it is that I have
done. This I see as the ultimate sentimentalism of people
increasingly desperate for a link, a connection with something — correction, with *anything*, that makes some sense. A
country which has based itself absolutely on the sacred
belief in sundered, severed, truncated, fractured, split,
divided, separate selves now craves a detailed account of my
development in the deluded hope that once all the facts are
known the odd case that I am will swim into focus, there will
be an intermingling, an intermeshing of parts and their
insanity will be miraculously proved to be wise policy. It is a
poisonous, romantic notion. In return I am offered freedom.
It's an offer which is positively presumptuous since they

suppose freedom is theirs to give. I thought I'd had the dreadful luck to land in the hands of the police, but it is far worse than that: I have fallen among philosophers. What's more, they are obsessed with hygiene in a very special way I've not come across since Jack Wyner lunched off the floor of his swimming pool. They plan to give me a shower.

Rich Jack Wyner! Not one but *two* garden boys, Freddie and Amos, who slouched around the garden sweltering in thick blue overalls and old felt hats; Freddie mowing the lawn and watering the ranunculi, Amos tending the pool, draining, scrubbing, plugging the cracks, fishing out leaves, putting in fresh chlorine three times a week. The swimming area was grassed and enclosed by a wooden trellis. In one corner, near the deep end, was a pumphouse, and in the other, an apple tree. Night and day the pump went, pushing the water through the filter, back into the pool, frothing out of a pipe set into the lowest of the steps in the shallow end. Entire water change each day (each hour?) Anyway, whichever, Wyner was damn proud of that filter. The pumphouse, bedded into the corner, bunker style, had a flat roof a foot or so off the ground, ideal for stretching out in the sun and catching your first summer tan.

I didn't need the sun, due to my condition, but Yannovitch, a Yugoslav with a milky, freckled skin, swore by it — the angle of the pumphouse roof gave even exposure to the right solar rays, or something like that. I'd have said that he tanned badly, couldn't take the sun. I'd have said so — but for the fact that I seldom talked about skin conditions or suntans. Seldom, if ever . . .

"Old Amos gets our pool so damn clear I swear that you could eat off the bottom!"

Jack Wyner was forever rabbiting on about his hygienic pool. One day, when his folks were out and the pool empty and freshly scrubbed, he'd done just that. No plates, nothing. Straight off the cold stone: knife, fork, napkin — the lot; he'd enjoyed cold meats and salads. Just goes to show. It seems the salads spread themselves around the place a bit, but he managed.

Smoothly rounded Wyner, softly pink all over, much of his face carpeted with fine white down years after the rest of us began shaving. This showed up suddenly when the sun was behind him. Fat Jack, seal-sleek, smooth as a bar of new soap, and smelling, so faintly that you almost didn't notice it, of sick. Three ovals piled up: bottom, belly and head, this last capped by a slick of hair so well greased the comb-teeth paths set hard from ear to ear in perfect curves. His legs dropped out of beautifully cut natty off-white shorts, too long by far, with zippered money pocket, button-down back pocket and no turn-ups. Slightly wet but luckily rich, his means made up for his dampness. An open, honest, anxious guy who'd begun life as a class schloep, a toady, before he'd come over to us, the bad eggs of the class, the boys, as old Donally put it, from 'rough surroundings': Rick van Dam, John Yannovitch, Theo Shuckel and myself, give or take one or two others, hangers-on and easily shaken off.

Most afternoons, except for Wednesdays, along with some of the girls from the Convent of Our Lady of Sorrows, we'd go swimming at old Wyner's shack up on the Ridge. A damned sight better than risking the public baths, a real pit of a place, used during the week only by snotty-nosed infants and octogenarians in bathrobes and purple rinses whose first impulse on entering the water was to piss the place yellow as jaundice. The Superintendent fought back with double-strength chlorine. Result? Open your eyes under water and you went blind for five minutes, arriving home with flamingo-pink eyes that would have done an albino proud.

Big Dottie Baker, incredibly well-developed and kind with it, a gentle, moony face, looking rather like the Queen Mother, all face-powder and soft, round creases, was there on those afternoons at Wyner's. Mary Smithson came too, when she felt like it. A nervous, fidgety girl inclined to jump at the least sound with a giggle that was almost a squeak, but not unpleasant. Jet black hair, very slender, a bit flat maybe, but her face was fantastic with large blue-grey eyes. She never said much and little at all when other people were speaking, but the eyes watched, darting this way and that, less eyes than strange tropical fish that swam in her face. Every so often I caught the eyes on me, though they'd flicked past my ears and were gone the instant I noticed them. Everybody knew that she loved herself. So what? She was exquisite. And then there was Mina Meintjies, as often as not, who spent a lot of time sitting on the steps of the shallow end where the inlet pipe bubbled, keeping her eyes open.

About four o'clock, hot for September, my arms folded carefully across my chest, and the sun dead centre on my back. Yannovitch slept on the pumphouse roof. Shuckel and Dottie sat at the deep end of the pool, their legs dangling in the water, saying nothing. Conversation was never Theo's strong point. You could barely see his forehead under his thick red hair. His face was choked up with freckles. Good at brooding, old Shuckel. Some girls found him sort of intense. Often it made them want to mother him. Maybe deep down they knew what he was — just an incredibly slow guy, with the makings of an intellectual. He read all his father's books. Rumour had it that his folks had taught him to speak German.

Van Dam was the only one swimming. Probably because Mary was still in the water, alone in a rounded corner of the pool with her arms flung out behind her on the stone lip, beautiful white wings, with her wet hair pushed behind her ears, delicately treading water. Whenever she allowed her legs to drift near the surface I'd see them through the clear water, moving shakily. Seeing her at rest, maybe even attentive, must have decided van Dam that the time had come to impress.

Even though I knew van Dam in those days as my good friend, if not my best, who would deny that he could be incredibly stupid? For one thing he set this huge store by prowess. He was a husky guy, inches taller than the rest of us and almost a foot over Yannovitch (a sore point that) with a fine head of hair. Dutch yellow, Yannovitch called it. A useful jibe. At his most boring van Dam wanted you to know all the time what a big deal he was.

"Hey Moto! Any of you guys — how many lengths of this bath can you swim under water, hey? You go fifteen with me? Bet you can't. Ah Jeez, man! Listen, I'm tired of these old games. Why don't we play something new? Ever tried hockey with golf clubs, or golf soccer? Don't say you won't when you mean you can't. S'easy. I'll be captain, okay?"

Trouble was he couldn't keep up with his own variations.

8

It was hell being caught out by van Dam, off the wall, ". . . one bounce, left-handed, and that is *out!* Or have you forgotten the *rules*?" — Disagree, and there went the ball, whap! into the rosebeds. He'd wipe his watering eyes, climb onto his bike and go home without another word. A bad loser.

The water was thrashing worse than a shark attack, gouts of it thudding into the corners of the bath. I gathered that van Dam was attempting that difficult and exhausting stroke known as the butterfly. From a drowning position a couple of inches below the surface he would jump into the air with a tremendous kick, flinging his arms forward. He was seldom airborne more than a moment before gravity took him by the short and curlies and he'd bellyflop and sink, his hair floating weirdly. In all, a flight of maybe eight inches. Luckily I didn't have to watch. A choking grunt as he left the water and the impact of his return kept me posted. Pretty soon he was spending most of the time submerged. Obviously he was well on the way to drowning. There was consolation in that. And Mary's eyes were closed.

In a world where every prospect pleased, only Kenny Darling propping up the gate was vile, in khaki shirt and shorts of the white-hunter variety, floppy khaki hat, green lining around the inside brim, reading . . . *Lives of the Saints* or *The Acts of the Apostles.* He wangled himself into these swimming afternoons on the strength of having been close to Wyner before he came over to us.

At school they said he couldn't swim. Van Dam, whose mother was friendly with Darling's old lady, said that his body was terribly disfigured by a huge purple birthmark stretching from nave to chaps, or somewhere, and he was too embarrassed to strip. As far as I could see he just came along to disapprove. A runty, thin sort of chap with the strangest skin, bluey-white it was, colour of swimming pool water, with a sheen to it as if it were pulled too tight, and almost transparent. If the sun got to it, red boils grew on nose and neck and it flamed in red patches, dropping off in chunks.

"To look at him, you'd imagine that if you got really close and peered you'd see his insides moving about — like those clocks in glass cases, y'know, with their workings grinding away." Shuckel told me this quite seriously. "Except that nobody will find out. He's so completely horrible from the outside — who's going to get up really close and *stare*? Not counting you, Moto old chap, who are Arab enough for anything. Care to take a peek?"

"Thanks a lot."

"Don't mention it."

Shuckel knew how wary I was on the subject of skin. Everybody knew it. Not that my skin was at all sensitive, you understand. Alas, no. But inside my skin I was sensitive. Shuckel gave way to these flights of fancy without a smile. If Kenny showed up at the pool, Yannovitch'd spend some time barracking him from his roost on the pumphouse roof.

"What! Not swimming, Mother's Little . . .?"

We had these names for him: "Mother's Little" or "Mommy's Little", also, "Little Darling", after the song they were playing a lot on the radio.

"Grab your costume, Little Darlin'. Paddle your tootsies. Be my guest. Or is it your time of the month?"

Maybe we were too hard on Little Darlin'. He was kind to me once. On a stinking afternoon, we had been making mercury barometers in the science lab, having been kept late after school and I'd slipped out to keep an appointment for a bit of nose to nose with this big giver called Jennifer Katz, behind the cricket pavilion. They said she was more precocious than most, being Jewish. An incredibly pretty girl, her father had said that she wasn't going to marry no ruddy goy. That's why he sent her to the convent: Catholics didn't count. Jennifer was making the most of things before she went off to join the Israeli army. She let me french-kiss her but held my hands tightly all the time.

While I was about my business, Brother Donally ambled back into the lab after a couple of quick nips in his room. Of course he called for me. The wise guys on the back benches were betting on the method of my execution. Mommy's Little covered up for me with the most professional lie ever heard, Shuckel said afterwards.

"Moto suddenly turned pale, Brother, began retching. First thought was that he'd inhaled evaporating mercury. As class monitor I ordered him out of the class immediately, Brother, and down to the cricket field, where he is recovering now, taking deep breaths. I hope I did right, Brother?"

"That Kenny's a fine monitor," Brother Donally beamed

when I slunk back, "quick and mature in a crisis. A good man in a shellhole, to be sure."

He'd been shell-shocked in one of the wars, I don't know which, and wore a steel plate in his forehead. His left eye wandered wildly and he was palpably insane. He couldn't have cared less about my condition, but he would never have forgiven himself if he'd not been in at the death . . .

"Feeling better, are you?"

"Yes thank you, Brother."

"Don't worry yourself, Moto. There's always a next time."

Darling's saintliness was sickening. He served at the Church of the Resurrection the early mass at six-thirty all through the week, first mass on Sunday and then acted as coin collector and usher at all the others. After receiving communion, his hands folded at his chest, his eyes screwed up, blundering into people, cocking his head towards the choir gallery so that the light from the stained glass windows fell on his face, which, not having much colour of its own, changed like a traffic light, red to orange to green, he'd make his blind way back to his pew, there to fall on his knees and stay that way until the blessing, kneading his closed eyes with his fists.

I don't think that Little Darlin' ever got over Fatty Wyner's defection and he was always sucking up to him in the most nauseating fashion. Once when Jack was going on in his usual way about the super hygiene of his swimming pool van Dam, who was feeling pretty mean that day, led him over to the poolside and pointed to little bits of green hairy algae beginning to sprout in tiny patches on the wall.

"There's breakfast growing down there, Wyner. Look! This nice little bit'd make mint sauce for Sunday lunch."

Wyner got very upset and rushed around yelling for Amos to come and clean away the gunge. That was when Mommy's Little stuck his oar in.

"Don't listen to him, Jack. If your pool grows mould you can be sure it's *clean* mould. Rather like penicillin. If you don't believe me I'll eat some just to prove it."

"I believe you, Kenny," Wyner said gratefully.

With my arches on the hard lip of the pool, in pain, I swayed backwards and forwards hoping the exercise would do some good. My arches had been falling for years: from

Gothic to Roman and then to such an all-time low that when I ran barefoot on a flat surface they slapped along like pieces of steak.

Van Dam had given up trying to be a butterfly and was standing in the centre of the pool with water pouring from his nose and ears, trying to retch quietly.

The sun was setting behind the apple tree and the lengthening shadows were beginning to chill the pool. But nobody moved. Shuckel and Dottie continued to brood side by side, paddling their feet. Mary rested on arms outstretched along the pool lip, trailing her legs of seaweed, head back, gazing blindly into the sun, her hair smoothed along her temples, shining, a seal just surfaced. Freddie had the sprinkler going on the lawn on the other side of the trellis fence and a little breeze carried the smell of wet earth and grass. I felt for a moment that if everybody agreed on it, things could stay like that forever.

In fact, as things turned out, I was wiser than I knew. I was never again at Jack Wyner's swimming pool. After that the dark forces took over and my separate development began. This is a statement of endings. It is produced by a voice from the past. All my endings are here except the last and I would have said that the last might have been left to the imagination were it not for the clear instruction, often repeated since I began writing, that nothing is to be left to the imagination. *Nothing.* Very well, then, the least I can do is to hold them to that: I shall write until I drop.

Mina was perched about two feet from me, water up to her shoulder, sitting on the step directly above the inlet pipe which boiled and frothed up between her legs. The pipe gave out purified water with enough force to buoy you up for a few moments if you sat on the bubbling column. The bubbles bombarding the legs were a pleasant sensation. We all did it now and then. Mina did it all the time. Shuckel suggested that she was sex-starved and this was her way of catching a cheap thrill. She was a bony sort, prim, with a clear complexion and a square mouth. A *nice* girl, my mother said. High praise. The skin across her face was tight and showed off her cheekbones to disadvantage. Unlike the other girls she always wore a bathing cap when she swam. White, tight and sensible, she was forever yanking it down over her ears with a rubbery squeak, tucking away a stray lock. It was always a shock when she took off the cap and shook loose her hair to see that it was long and quite beautifully blonde. After the bathing cap it didn't seem to belong to her. I thought of her as all skull.

On top of the pumphouse, which was the only place left with good sun on it, Yannovitch slept. His folks had come from Yugoslavia to South Africa with nothing, and as far as I could see they still had nothing, though they ate well. Stews I'd never tasted before, and wine with every meal. A yellowish wine, tart, and served very cold from a carafe by his old man who smiled a lot and spoke no English. "Cheapest place to get smashed in town," Shuckel said. He could be totally heartless. Mrs Yannovitch spoke English all the time very well, and was a dumpling, only much, much larger and she'd hug us before, during and after the huge meals she set before us. The Yannovitchs had this crazy way with their servants. They didn't seem to know the first damn thing about *apartheid*. A family of them lived in the backyard rooms. They often ate in the kitchen and seemed to share the house.

"It's bloody embarrassing," van Dam complained, "to go to the pisshouse only to find this dirty great coon's beaten you to it and you know he's used it because he's still buttoning up when he comes out. Obviously they've got no idea how to treat their servants . . . coming from Yugoslavia."

The Yannovitchs drove an old green, hump-back Dodge to Sunday mass. Parked in among the Vauxhalls and Morrises it looked like a kaffir taxi.

"Before my folks bought it, it *was* a kaffir taxi," Yannovitch said calmly when I told him this, "and it's gone down since we got it."

He knew how to start the Dodge with silver paper and he used to steal it on the weekends and take us for late night hamburgers at the Swiss Cottage Roadhouse. I'm sure that his folks must have known, but they pretended not to notice because they were both crazy about little Johnny and pleased that he was hanging around with Shuckel, van Dam and me. Mainly, I suspect, because they thought we were all good Anglo-Saxon boys. Meanwhile, we were a Teuton, a Dutchman

13

and only God knows what I was.

Yannovitch did not enthuse when I told him how I felt about Mary.

"There's rocks in your head, Moto."

"She's been giving me the eye."

"Crap. You don't know what day of the week it is. That big guy — drum-major in the bugle band ... what's his name? Trevor Goble — don't you know, she's got the hots for Goble? Everybody knows that. Anyways she doesn't give ice in winter. None of these convent girls give. You want to get a babe from the Southern Suburbs, like me. Do they go it! Hoowha!" He clicked his fingers and licked his lips.

"I'm going to ask her to the Matric Dance."

"You've lost your marbles. Anyway, you can't dance. You'll end up flat on your arse."

"I'll learn."

"Oh yes — " his lip drooped so much that I saw two of his bottom teeth clearly — "I can just see you ... toddling off to Tommy Williams' Dance Studios, Saturday morning, pushing a couple of pongy bags around the room, slow, slow — Wait! What's this? Gram's stopped. Wind it up again. Right. On we go — quick, quick, slow . . ."

"Wake up, Yannovitch, she's beautiful."

He shook his head. "Not my type. I like knockers. A good pair. Something to hold on to." He pushed me in the chest. "Maybe you don't care about that. Maybe you're big enough for both of you?" He stuck his right hand up in the air and scratched his armpit. "Ha, bloody ha!"

"Anybody who is happy with the plain average is going to be offhand about excellence."

"Oh balls."

I stood on the edge of the pool punishing my arches on the stone lip, teetering there, setting up a rhythm. Fixing my eyes on the bubbles surging up in a fizzing swarm beneath Mina, I began my special chest-expanding exercises, being careful to keep my arms folded so the elbows covered my twin chests. They were my greatest problem. The colour of my skin was bad enough. Maybe, I admitted to myself in the small hours, I wasn't a white man at all. Maybe I was a coloured — or a mulatto (a word I preferred because it at least had a ring to it); a coloured, O.K. — but a coloured with

14

breasts? Now I mean to say that physically, in the *manly* sense, I was orthodox. One might even have described the area of my chest as nicely broad. But the fact was that my breastbone divided my front like a river running between two low hills. Seen from the side, which is mostly the way I saw myself in front of the mirror, I was struck, and struck damn often let me say, by the fact (facts) of what were, well . . . breasts. Nothing major, you understand, or in the least pneumatic, or *sagging*. But a pair of small ones, certainly, on either side of my breastbone, fleshy hillocks (hummocks?), mounds, anyway, gently swelling things topped by nipples. It didn't much help knowing that otherwise I was fairly normal: for God's sake I was even shaving my moustache and I positively bulged out of my swimming costume, a small men's of course, in order to advertise, AND at the last measurement in the bogs at school during small break I'd found I had half an inch on Yannovitch. Quite something . . . still the *facts* remained. The moment I took off my shirt my bosoms knocked hell out of every credential I could muster.

I got desperate and told my mother.

"Don't you know that adolescents always have trouble with growing glands Harry?" she asked pleasantly. "I hope you're not thinking that you can do without your glands."

I developed little concealments; hung my towel around my neck when we were swimming so the ends kept the old bust under cover. Or I folded my arms, and always sunbathed lying on my stomach. Even so, the word spread. Guys used to cycle past my place shouting. "Come on out, Jane Russell!" and "Give us a feel, Harry!" My mother finally got the message and took me along to a doctor who diagnosed something that sounded like one of the seven deadly sins; it was called *Pectus Excavatum*.

"Clack's the name, rhymes with quack. Sunken sternum. Not an unusual condition, though notable in your case. Will go on as the chest fills out. Can be helped by exercise. Wherever you are, exercise. Think of yourself as a steam train, a dirty great locomotive, heavily loaded and starting up a steep hill: Deep breath in through the nose, now h-o-l-d it! Then out, s-l-o-w-l-y . . . choof-choof-choof . . . Do they tease you much at school?"

15

"No, no, not very much." I caught my mother's eye. She frowned and I knew she was about to tell him about the Jane Russell gag. "Well, sometimes I'm asked my bra size."

That was one my mother hadn't heard. She gasped.

Dr Clack laughed gently to himself. "It's a funny old world. Half the young ladies who come to see me would give their eye-teeth to have your problem."

He produced a bottle of thick, black, gluey syrup. "Apply to the offending parts morning and night. But rub in well because the stuff stains."

That was true enough. It stained. It stained right through my vest and shirt front — in the middle of geography, we were discussing the Detroit automobile industry, I remember — and there appeared quite quickly, like developing pictures, two black ghastly advertisements for my secret shame. Shuckel was entranced. "It's just like the Holy Shroud!"

Winters were all right. I was decently swaddled. But summers brought in fresh surprises. I worked at my exercises as religiously as I prayed to Jesus, Mary and Joseph that I wouldn't die suddenly in state of mortal sin and roast in hell for ever. I puffed my all on the bus, in church, while I ate, in the classroom and in the bogs. If I remembered to keep the choof-choofs to myself then it was a secret exercise. But I did not always remember and I suppose it was this that got Mina Meintjies interested enough to look my way.

Choof! She bobbed among the bubbles like a ping-pong ball. Then her face, usually taut-skinned and flat, had an accident. It was rather like the way in which a perfect beach hit by a sudden wave is wrenched; her mouth opened really wide, her teeth stood out over her lower lip and her googly eyes slid down to my waist somewhere. *Choof*?

My bathing costume had this pretty loose elastic around my waist and the thighs, well, groin, actually, and I had the horrible thought that maybe the elastic had perished or something, or the strain of chest and arch exercises combined with the fact that it was the cozzie designed for a stripling pressed into the service of well-endowed Harry Moto had done it, or undone it. Anyway, when I looked where Mina was looking, there was a well-known head with its circumcised collar pushed enquiringly into the world. From where I was standing it seemed to me the sort of look a tortoise might wear, enquiring and cautious. There it was for all the world to see, dream of virgins, terror of mothers superior, absolute rebuttal of my girlish chests. Pushed enquiringly, I say, when seen from above with an owner's fond eye. From Mina's point of view, who knows, it might have been more true to say that it thrust *brutally*, or aimed, or even, if she had any imagination, leered and winked? Maybe she saw it doing all these things at once, and all at HER?

Under other circs, O.K. . . . I mean natch, I'd like to have shown *everything* I had to every girl I knew so that she would be happy and dream of what fate had in store for her. But it was not the right place. The run-up was wrong, the angle bad, the light failing, my audience not ready. I looked at Mina. She looked at me but not in the eye. Oh no! She wouldn't do the decent thing and look away for even a second, time enough for me to manage a quick tuck for decency. Obviously I couldn't stand there fumbling with myself while her eyeballs bulged as badly as I'm sure Bernadette's did when Shazam! the Virgin Mary popped out of the rocky cleft at Lourdes. One sound from Mina, a movement and the others would all see it. And since, unlike the Virgin Mary, I couldn't disappear, pouf! I did the next best thing. I dropped like a stone. Mina's scream followed me into the water.

Afterwards when we'd all changed, we had tea in the garden, with Jack plying us with chocolate éclairs and Coke. The girls wore their convent tunics, shapeless, navy blue affairs with complicated drawstrings which when pulled tight at the neck gave them the look of those bags of Magaliesberg pipe tobacco, dark, greasy and pungent, which I bought to empty out the *twak* and keep my marbles in. Mary sat next to me and when she moved I half expected to hear the click of glass behind the cotton cloth. The other guys had changed back into school uniforms, khaki shorts and white shirts. I was wearing my Bobby Locke short-sleeved golf shirt in canary yellow I'd especially brought along in my satchel. Mary settled in her chair and licked chocolate off her éclair with a soft quick little tongue right there beside my ear.

"How nicely you tan, Harry. You're browner than any of us."

I stared at the arm she touched trying to believe it really

belonged to me.

Mina made a noise in her nose like budgies kissing. "It's nothing great, you know — Harry's case. In fact there are thousands that wouldn't give you twopence for it. He has a natural tan. It's not something he tries for."

"A permanent tan," van Dam offered.

"A touch of the tarbrush," Yannovitch declared.

Mina shrieked at that and threw up her hands in front of her face. But I saw she peered at me through her fingers.

I let it pass, very conscious of Mary's hand resting on my arm and not daring to move in case I disturbed it. I felt intense, blood-pounding gratitude to Bobby Locke. I was amazed by the fetching way in which the cheerful shirt-sleeve circled the bicep contrasting beautifully with the smooth brown arm. I flexed the arm to get the muscle up and then leaned back very casually, leaving the bicep centre-stage as it were.

"I think they're jealous," Mary said.

Van Dam gurgled. "Jealous! Listen. Let me tell you that when Harry first came to my place my mother thought he must be looking for work. She was on the point of offering him a job as a garden boy."

"Shame on you boys — " Dottie's lip trembled — "You shouldn't make jokes about people looking like natives."

"No, that's right," van Dam nodded gravely, "the natives might not like it."

Mother's Little, whose heart pumped custard at the least opportunity, chipped in. "A man has his dignity." Unwisely he pointed his finger at Yannovitch. "No matter what colour his skin is."

Darling's mother had made him silly in this way. Six foot in her socks, bosom like a streamroller, she was active in the Catholic Women's League, fiend of the Cake and Candy Sales, and went about doing good with an iron will, succouring widows and so on. I had seen her at the weekly demonstrations held on the traffic island outside the University protesting against *apartheid*, standing with all the other old hens, heads dropped over their placards. Hers read: "*I am a little black baby. In 3 Months I will die of Malnutrition.*"

"Shut up Mommy's Darling. Another peep out of you and I'll break your skull and pour out the juice like a cokey-nut."

I don't know why he mispronounced that word. I'd told him a dozen times. Anyway, Darling got the message. He stood up without a word and walked outside onto the stoep where his bike was parked, took out his pump and pumped the tyres Yannovitch as per usual had let down.

"Shame," Dottie murmured. "Why are you so horrible to him? He'll go home now."

"Good," said Yannovitch. "It's past his bath-time."

The question of skin colour had surfaced in my mind about the age of ten and grew steadily more menacing. It was an issue for me long before van Dam's mother made her now famous mistake of taking me for a potential garden boy in search of a job. It worried my mother and father. It was never something we could discuss over the breakfast table — though it lay between us, somewhere above the salt and to the left of the marmalade, all the days of my boyhood. For years my mother had tried to stop me swimming in summer on the grounds that I had a "delicate" skin. In fact I had a tough, buff hide that darkened in the sun with a slight mottling effect rather like bamboo. My father, on the other hand, explained my rusty colour in terms of the bad influence of my friends. If I spent every waking hour hanging around with swarthy dagoes, wops and eyties (he meant Yannovitch) then, he told my mother, she should expect something to rub off, in much the same way that dog-owners grew to look like their hounds. I decided I must be some sort of a throwback. The thing was to find out where the fault began. I started a secret investigation of my family. My father and mother provided no clues. She was very pale with black hair shot with grey. He was fat and pink to the point of greyness. Both utterly kosher then by all prevailing norms. Luckily, we didn't have many relations. There was Uncle Ferdie who travelled in his Opel Car-a-van for Elizabeth Arden and smelt amazingly good. I had read of boys whose cherished memory in later life was of mother dripping in furs and perfume stooping over the drowsy child for a goodnight kiss on her way out to a grand ball. My mother never wore perfume because it gave my father asthma. But I remember Uncle Ferdie, red-necked, a proper European, who used to visit us on his half-day with his spruce little Ronald Coleman mustache and centre parting, with his hair slicked so brightly across his scalp it seemed painted on and all of him always heavy with the fumes of lager and Blue Grass. There was, too, my mother's sister, Auntie Denys, who lived alone in Brakpan though she had a succession of friends whom I was always told to call Uncle: Uncle Kim, Uncle Rollo, Uncle Mannie. I liked Auntie Denys because when I was small she'd swing me up on her broad lap and in her hoarse whisky voice would shout: "Up, up, little man, and rest your curly head upon my *numbies!*" And with that she'd bang my wiry mop between her breasts which always made the uncles laugh and my father say we had to leave. There remained only my Gran, my father's mother who lived in an old age home in a distant suburb called Cedar Grove. There never had been any cedars out there, never would be, but perhaps taking the wish for the deed the area was settled in great numbers by Lebanese immigrants. In Gran I found the link. Gran with her manly, hairy chin and skin the texture of chamois leather, brown fading into yellow. We were two of a kind and loved each other, often taking long walks through the dusty little suburb. She doted on me. "What a handsome little man Harry is," she told my father. "Who'd have thought your child would turn out so good-looking, Graham. Of course, he has your complexion." And my father, furious, would turn away muttering helplessly. Gran and I took walks among the soft, olive Lebanese who of course knew instantly the special case we were and they'd wink and whisper and point behind our backs. "Bloody darkies," Gran said comfortably, "they'll overrun the whole world one day, Harry. Mark my words." And the little hairs on her chin quivered in anticipation of the great victory.

The shadows had begun to lengthen over the pool, changing it from green to a colder, deeper blue tinged with violet and indigo. Mary's hand fluttered on my arm which had completely seized up by this time for lack of movement. It stirred and left, taking off with a gentle touch on the elbow in parting. "Never mind what they say. I like you as you are."

   "Oh, Harry's fine," van Dam allowed. "I'll say this. He'll be all right when the revolution comes."

20

"There won't be one," Yannovitch said flatly.

"Oh yes? Says who?"

"Stands to reason. In the first place, nothing ever happens around here. And secondly, who'd clear up the mess afterwards?"

"Oh yes," Mina said, "Harry'll be all right when the revolution comes. It's just that I don't see how he's going to hold out till then. That's the trouble with Harry."

2

People say that things are so bad here they make you want to spit. I spat once. I spat in a bus, dead centre of the upstairs aisle, beneath a large sign painted in black letters on the creamy enamel wall above the front windows expressly forbidding it:

Prevent T.B. Do Not Spit
Moenie Spoeg Nie Asseblief

One lived, of course, surrounded by such signs and notices. Most of them, however, served some clear purpose, the point of which everyone recognised as being essential for their survival: WHITES ONLY on park benches; BANTU MEN HERE on nonwhite lavatories; or INDIAN BENCH; or DEFENCE FORCE PROPERTY: PHOTOGRAPHS FORBIDDEN; or SECOND-CLASS TAXI; or THIS PLAYGROUND IS RESERVED FOR CHILDREN OF THE WHITE GROUP. And, of course, people were forever being prosecuted for disobeying one or other of these instructions. But I'd never ever seen anyone spitting on a bus. People must have done it, I supposed. Somewhere there must have been gangs who made it a habit to climb aboard, buy a ticket as innocent as the day is long, and then start hurling their tubercular gob around the place. But seeing is believing and I never saw anyone do it. So I claim a record.

That day I take to be rather special in my life. Firstly, I exposed myself to Mina Meintjies. Then I spat in the bus. The two things were not connected except in time and degree of embarrassment and I can't truly say that I meant to do either, but it must have looked that way to the watching world and as Dekker likes to put it: "Meaning is what other people makes of things." Looking back, I think perhaps these things were signs that I was about to leave the great white camp in which I'd spent sixteen unhappy years. My separate development was about to begin. Harry Moto, the strangely brown kid with breasts, flat feet and funny hair was on his way out. I took some consolation from the knowledge that Mina, on the evidence of her own eyes, had to admit that I wasn't as black as I'd been painted. This came out over tea at Wyner's place when Yannovitch talked of "Harry's terrifying tan."

"I'll bet," said Mina, turning the lemon's head full on me and showing eyes like slits, "that parts of him are as white as you or me." And the slits gleamed. It's a terrible thing — a lemon with eyes.

My father took a similarly consoling view of what he called "nature's intentions" concerning my body when he caught me trying to measure my breasts in front of the bathroom mirror with the pink tape-measure I'd filched from my mother's sewing basket. "Leave yourself alone, boy," he instructed me sharply. "You're just as normal as Nature intended you to be, no better or worse: we are planted in her garden and must grow according to her plan."

I've thought of Nature ever since as a kind of second-rate garden boy.

My father was always fond of telling me how lucky I was. I had been given so much. My mother used to back him up by asking me sadly if I had any idea how little one truly needed in this world. My father usually misunderstood what she meant and thought he was being got at and they'd have a fight. Afterwards he'd go back to his original point. "You've never lacked for a single thing, Harry," he would insist regularly, emphasising each word with a peculiar little bobbing motion of his chin which was large, round and shiny in surprising contrast to the rest of his long grey face, and made him look not unlike a recently blown light-bulb. His globular chin reminded me of the ball dancing above the words of a song at the bioscope. "Name a single thing you've ever lacked." The chin bounced expectantly.

"An identity card."

He smiled encouragingly. "There is too much bureaucracy in this world as it is."

Van Dam always made a point of carrying his ID around. "If the natives are forced to carry passes," he explained, "I think the least we Europeans can do is to carry our ID cards. It shows that we are also penalised for our colour. I'm not for *apartheid*, mind you, but I think you have to admit people are different."

"What a load of bullshit," Yannovitch told him. "Africans have to carry passes because people think they're inferior, not because they're different."

"They *are* different," van Dam said stubbornly.

"What's the difference?"

"Well, they're black and we're white — for a start. There's no getting around that."

"Excuse me," Wyner chipped in, "but there are ways of getting around that. I mean, take Nat King Cole. My dad says that Nat King Cole is a real white man. He says Nat King Cole can sleep in our house any day of the week."

"Oh, it's no good telling van Dam things like that," said Yannovitch. "He believes in differences. I mean just say Nat King Cole *did* come to your place, Wyner, and you said to him — 'Come on old Nat, give us a song' — well, as sure as shooting he'd have just begun, say, 'Dinner for one, please James,' and in would burst van Dam demanding to see his pass."

We often had these conversations about colour and ID cards but I tended to keep out of them, never feeling there was anything I could decently add. The ID card was a stippled green plastic rectangle about four inches by three, showing a grainy snapshot of the owner and his registration number, followed by a capital W for "White". At one time there were fears of forgeries among unscrupulous non-Europeans "trying for White", and the Government considered using a double-check system: the idea was to tattoo the ID number on the wrists or forearms of all *bona fide* Europeans with a special invisible ink developed by a Cape wine farmer, Tony "Babelas" van Breda from the skin of the Tokai grape. The number showed up only under infra-red light and the idea was that once the population had been tattooed, teams of inspectors equipped with portable scanners would police the system by making random checks among ID card carriers. Everyone agreed that van Breda's ink had enormous commercial possibilities in such areas as laundry marking and sensitive correspondence and he had gone so far as to market the stuff under the slogan, "The Ink That Thinks!" Several Junior Chambers of Commerce had elected him "Man of the Year" and people were openly saying that here was another Sampie de Doorns, legendary inventor of the Gloria Sunshine Skin Lotion and Bleaches empire. On the other hand the English papers attacked the plan. They declared that tattooing was a form of mutilation, a barbaric practice more appropriate to the Africans from whom we Whites were attempting to distinguish ourselves by carrying ID cards. Besides, they wrote, this was the thin end of the wedge and if tattooing with Babelas Ink were not opposed in the name of liberty, the day was not far off when we would all be expected to walk around with bones through our noses. This reaction from the English press made the Government really keen to push on with the scheme and the Minister put out a statement claiming that an invisible tattoo was a small price to pay for the preservation of Western Christian civilisation at the Southern tip of the African continent. People who opposed the plan were all homosexual Jewish communists who should go and live in Ghana.

In fact, in the end the plan failed. What killed it was the discovery that with the application of Babelas Ink to human flesh, a chemical reaction took place, whether of the infra-red rays with the ink, or the ink with perspiration was never decided. It was found among the team of prison warders who had volunteered as guinea pigs "in the interests of safeguarding our national and cultural heritage and combating communism" (so read the statement issued by the Prison Officers' Association) that the treated area of the upper arm became swollen and painful. Even then, it looked as if the Government would press ahead, arguing that this was a small price to pay for an infallible system of registering authentic Europeans, had it not been that the severe blistering of the skin made the numbers difficult to read. The tattooing plan was reluctantly scrapped and the Government settled for the green card and the power of rumour. The plastic card had been specially treated, the story went, so that if anyone tried to tamper with it, the card would somehow know and turn black, or shrivel up, or release a poisonous gas.

When you turned sixteen you were eligible for a card. Photographers came around to the school and took pictures. I hid in the lavatory all day. Thing was you couldn't have your picture taken for the card until you produced the official form showing your family tree. My father somehow never got the form. He was always about to collect it from the Registration Office in town, but either got there too early and the office hadn't opened, or too late and it had "just shut", or he arrived there, he would tell me, "at exactly the time I should have done: I stood in the queue for an hour only to have the window slammed in my face because the clerk was going to lunch."

My mother would nod understandingly at this. She knew all about queues and clerks because she worked behind the counter in the Post Office. "It makes you want to spit, doesn't it Graham? On the other hand, fair is fair, even clerks are human, they have to eat and you don't object to a clerk having lunch, do you Graham? I'm sure even you stop to eat sometimes . . ."

I waited a long time for my bus. There weren't many buses up on the Ridge. The locals didn't need them. Either you went out in a Jag or a Lincoln Continental or you never left the house. I was joined at the bus stop by a fat woman in a pair of tight black slacks that hooked under the arches showing bulging calves, and a shocking pink blouse with sequins around the neck. She was carrying a packet of humbugs the size of a kitbag and held it as if it were a baby, nursing it in the crook of her arm, patting and smoothing the creases, and singing quietly into it.

Catching buses was a frustrating business at the best of times. Though there were different buses for Blacks and Whites one never knew until the last moment which was which as they all looked alike except for a small green board that hung in the driver's window and read "Non-Europeans Only". Three times the fat lady and I gathered ourselves, took our lives in our hands and stepped into the path of a swaying double-decker, waving madly, and three times the buses swerved past and pulled up twenty yards down the road where the Blacks had their separate stop.

The humbug woman got pretty mad. "It's all very well

having separate buses for Europeans and Bantu. Trouble is they use white drivers and conductors on the black buses and since there's more bloody Bantu than Whites, we don't get enough buses. The Bantu gets three to every one of ours. And also there's not enough staff around, so they got to take the lowest of the low, know what I mean? The dregs is what they gotta employ on the buses. Bladdy monkeys straight from the bush."

As things turned out this was a pretty fair description of the conductor who met us on the running board. Short and fat, he leaned out from the running board on one long arm sweating patchily into his navy serge uniform and chivvied us aboard, yanked the bell cord twice and the bus pulled off. That was the new signalling system. Once for a stop, twice for go, three times for emergency halt. It replaced the old system in which the conductor gave the same signals with loud blasts on a large silver whistle with a pea in it. God help you if you got in the way.

"Hang on to your suspenders, lady," he said.

The humbug woman gave me a significant glance. "What did I tell you? Straight down from the bloody trees, half of them."

The conductor scowled. He must have got the gist of this because he made several low passes with his ticket punch near my fly, clicking angrily. I saw the headlines: *Ticket Collector Castrates Schoolboy!!* Keeping an eye on the wicked chattering little silver punch I shot upstairs behind the fat lady who sat with the great bag of sweets on her knee, hugging it to her breast, muttering furiously to it. The conductor came down the aisle jingling his coin machine. He was more gorilla than monkey, I decided. The arms that hung to his knees ended in great fingers furred in black hair between his knuckles. He snapped his punch. I crossed my legs and gave him a florin. The coin machine spat change and he counted it from one big palm into the other. When the fingers touched I saw spiders mating. He got his sums wrong and puzzled over it, taking off his cap and rubbing the fistful of change in his hair. The coins he gave back to me were greasy, smelling hugely of Vaseline Hair Oil.

The bus gathered speed down the long hill. There was no one at the lower stops and the driver seemed determined to make the most of his clear run. The rivets in the steel walls began creaking. I looked around. The conductor leaned up against the stairwell casually riffling the tightly packed wads of tickets in his belt. A few old men in the back seats squeaked when we hit about fifty and after that it was all momentum. The conductor leaned against the stairwell clearly enjoying our fear.

In the face of his open scorn, scared as I was it was impossible to give the least sign of fear; no desperate grabbing of the seat rail in front of me, or anything like that. Result was I was being tossed about pretty sickeningly. My buttocks turned cowards early on and each tried independently for a purchase on the seat which the polished red leather wouldn't permit. I stared at the T.B. warning. If I were ever to get T.B., I decided, I would go and live quietly in the Karoo where they said the air was good for that sort of thing and there I would recover or die, but either way I would never be heard of again. On balance, I decided, I would prefer to die of T.B. than in some bus smash on the way home from Jack Wyner's place.

It was the humbug woman who took action. Gently placing her packet on the seat beside her and whispering to it to sit still, she stood up and yanked the leather bell-pull three times. The driver hit the brakes. With a great screaming of tyres and passengers the bus slowed and skidded to a halt. I was flung teeth first into the chromium rail of the fat lady's seat. In the back the old men were whinnying frantically. The lady slammed backwards in her seat, righted herself, replaced the packet on her lap and stared straight ahead of her. I looked around to see the conductor's head appearing above the stairwell down which he must have fallen. He had lost his cap and his hair covered his face, which was red and angry.

"Who done that? Who pulled the cord?"

"I did." The humbug woman gave a quiet triumphant smile.

"Are you crazy?" He jabbed a finger to his temple. "I went down those steps on my head, lady. I could've died! It's an offence, you know, to stop the bus. Only the conductor is allowed to signal an emergency stop . . ." His sonorous tone told us he was quoting from the regulations.

She turned to him and very deliberately lifted her right arm, pulled a gibbering face and scratched her armpit.

He tried a more indirect line. "The driver's very safe, even at speed. He knows what he's doing, take it from me. They get tested, these drivers. First they get an ordinary licence, then they get one for the bus, but only after they been tested. They don't give licences away, you know."

"No? Then I reckon he must have bought his at Woolworths." She smiled knowingly into her packet, took out a sweet and munched on it.

"She means he was going too fast. There would have been a smash."

He stared at me. Even with my help it was some time before the message made the long journey to his brain. He rubbed his hands in his hair. The silver punch started up its rikkitikkitavi routine.

"Oh yes? You sit there with your fancy yellow golf shirt and your funny crinkly hair thinking you're such a big deal. Let me tell you, with hair like that if I turned you upside down I'd have a terrific pot scourer. Oh yes, I couldn't buy better than you at Woolworths."

"Yes, he's a cheeky young chap," the humbug woman offered with her mouth full. "I knew it as soon as I clapped eyes on him. A student, I said. It's written all over his face." She had turned her coat with amazing suddenness. "There's no need for you to stick your spoke in, my boy. I can make my own complaints, thank you very much."

"I'm not a student," I said.

"What are you, then?"

"Bladdy students!" an old man shouted from the back of the bus. "Too big for their pants. Always shoving their spoke in; always wanting their tickey's worth."

"I'm just a schoolboy," I told her, "an ordinary schoolboy."

The conductor, I saw, was quite buoyed up by the growing support. He put his great hands on his knees and grinned at his audience. I sat back in my seat and watched his reflection in the chromium rail. Then I felt the huge furry spiders settle on my shoulder. "You know what I'm going to do with you, sonny boy? I'm going to ask you to get off my bus."

"You don't look like an ordinary schoolboy," the humbug

woman offered after staring at me carefully for a long while.

I shook off his hand. 'I didn't pull the bell. Why should I get off?" I folded my arms, sat back and concentrated on the "No Spitting" sign.

"You're getting off because I say so — and because if you don't they'll be selling you at Woolworths — as mincemeat in the cat food department." This got an appreciative laugh from the old men and I could tell that with the bus now solidly behind him the conductor was beginning to enjoy himself.

"But I've paid for another three stops."

"Listen, Crinklehead — for you the bus stops right here. Come to think of it, now that I look at you hard I don't know if you've got any right to be on this bus in the first place, sitting there so poncey in your bladdy yellow golf shirt, like a bladdy canary . . . Tweet! Tweet!" He stuck his thumbs in his ears and flapped his fingers like monstrous hairy wings. I felt the wind. "This bus is for Europeans only. Have you got an ID card, hey Crinklehead?"

I got up very slowly from my seat. The shot about the ID card had gone home. "All right. I'll go. But I'll complain about this. I'll write to the municipality."

"You can write to the bladdy Governor-General as far as I'm concerned," he returned amiably, convinced now that he'd won.

I made a last, despairing stab at saving a shred of dignity.

"And another thing — don't call me Crinklehead." If he allows me this, I thought, I'll go quietly. "Please."

"Cring-kul-head! Cring-kul-head!" the old men bawled.

I was moving slowly backwards, keeping my eyes on the conductor who watched me down the aisle snapping his thumbs through his packs of tickets and jingling his leather and silver harness like a bloody victory parade.

In his cab downstairs the driver had lost patience and the bus had begun to move. Reaching the end of the aisle I felt the support rail around the stairwell pressing into my back and suddenly I knew what I must do. I held up an imperious hand for silence, then leaning forward, conscious of the eyes of every passenger upon me I spat very carefully into the middle of the aisle.

I went down the steps two at a time. Behind me the air

was full of cries of "Sis!" I was on the pavement and twenty feet or more from the bus now pulling away at speed before the conductor arrived on the running board. I waved. He leaned out from the running board. For a moment I thought he was coming after me. I could see him contemplating the jump but he must have known he'd never make it, he so fat aɪ◆l locked into the heavy harness. He waved his fist above his head like a club. I could see him wrestling with his brain to give him the words that would best apply. "Yellow livered scum!" he tried for starters. Then "Filthy bastard!" But that didn't do, despite a little Swiss yodel he gave the final syllables to increase their range. Then, just as the bus moved out of earshot, cupping his hands around his mouth so his words would carry, he pulled out the plum. "White kaffir!"

His words carried very well. In fact they were positively bruited abroad. Passersby took the full force of them and stared at me. Worse still, after taking a good look, I'll swear some of them actually nodded.

He had a gift, that conductor — I see it now. He had great powers of definition. He was wasted on the buses, poor guy. The thing is that this entire country has always based itself on two propositions, to wit: that the people in South Africa are divided into separate groups according to their racial characteristics and that all groups are at war with each other. Before you're clear about your groups, you must be sure you're clear about your individuals. As they teach the kids to chant in the grades: "An impure group is a powerless group!" Or again, in the words of the old prayer, "If South Africa safeguards *apartheid*, *apartheid* will safeguard South Africa." Preserve the bloodlines. That was the rallying cry for generations. May your skin-tones match the great colour chart in the sky. Anyone who broke the blood lines, who wasn't on the chart, was a danger to the regular order of things. You fought such renegades, mutants, throw-backs and freaks with the power of definition. When in doubt, define. Once defined, the enemy could be classified, registered and consigned to one of the official, separate racial groups which give this country is uniquely rich texture. "White kaffir": the words have a ring to them. I came to be grateful for them. Up until then I hadn't any proper idea what I was. What the conductor gave me was an identity. Ever since, I've been an identity in search of a group.

"Look at what the cat's dragged in," my mother said. "Well, find something useful to do till suppertime. Don't wander about under my feet like a sick hen."

That was her way of talking; a rhetorical question followed by some observation which usually reflected badly on whomever she was addressing. She'd got into the habit over the years. It was partly compensation for the fact that nobody answered her questions and partly so that she could organise the world and keep it at bay. My mother had a horror of things being out of place. I didn't begrudge her this. She had to hold the ring. All too often my father and I had fights and she was the referee.

My father was a claims clerk in the All-Risks Department of a large insurance company. I've forgotten which it was at that time. He changed jobs half-a-dozen times in as many years. I was about twelve when I first realised that my father suffered a continuing tragedy in his career. He was a claims clerk who wanted to be a salesman.

"If I was a salesman I'd get a bigger salary and fat pickings from my commission, free use of the office car out of hours, free petrol at the weekends. We'd buy a bigger house, Molly. We'd get another girl to help you and a garden boy. Maybe a new house, up there on the Ridge where Harry's smart friends live, y'know. You could have a decent garden at last, instead of camping over a God-forsaken shale pit with funny chemicals in it, like poor Whites."

I'll grant him this — he really tried. He applied for and got jobs with insurance companies advertising for salesmen. But somehow, once there, he was shunted back into a glass office in the claims department. He practised selling life insurance to his friends. But there weren't many friends and once sold they were sold for life. When he was born the bad fairy stamped "All-Risks Clerk" on his brow and everybody read it there — in flaming letters — everybody but my father. Consequently, life was one long irritation.

Maybe he took it out on my mother when I was asleep. But during waking hours I was the target. If I smiled before breakfast, let my hair grow or breathed with my mouth open he'd suddenly go white around the lips and start yelling his head off. I'd yell back. So it went in that boring fashion. Sometimes, and it got so bad that I quite looked forward to these occasions because they broke the monotony, he'd pick up something heavy like an ashtray or a tyre lever and chase me around the house. My mother would rush out as we passed the kitchen window, shouting after us: "You two going at it hammer and tongs again? Like bloody kids, the pair of you."

I was used to my mother but my friends found her hard to deal with.

"So you're the Dutch boy?" she asked van Dam when he first came round to my place. "I suppose that you miss all those tulips — out here in South Africa? Still we've a much higher standard of living than you Hollanders are used to and you must be very grateful for that."

Van Dam was not pleased. His family had come to South Africa from Delft three generations before and he considered himself totally English.

Mind you, it suited me having my mother turn away my friends. There was nothing much doing at my place. Back and front of the house our quarter-acre was a wilderness of red shale: the front garden with its tiny strip of kikuyu grass hanging on with a leathery toehold, the line of drooping cannas against the fence, a few dying ranunculi beside the path.

My mother was cooking supper. Our girl, Charity, sat rocking in her chair at the door. I say girl, as a manner of speaking. She was sharp boned, surly, somewhere between thirty and menopause. Servant, too, is not right. Charity was anything but that. She sometimes did the washing, but stopped immediately she saw somebody watching her. My mother said that her sense of responsibility made her touchy. Charity felt that she ought to be trusted. If she thought we were checking up on her she became angry. When she was angry she did the cooking. Clicking her tongue over the pots on the stove she didn't care who watched then. Boiled fiercely a long while, steam blocking the windows, the potatoes crumbled, took in water like beach sand; carrots lost colour, grew as pale as stillborn mice, lying on the plate oozing a little orange fluid.

33

My father would look up from his plate when Charity had stomped back to the kitchen leaving us alone with our food steaming into our faces. "For God's sake, let her go," he'd beg my mother. "Ten years you've been training her to cook and she still serves us this hash."

"She doesn't cook — she declares war," I said, "let her go."

"What? And spend another ten years training the new girl to cook? I know you two, you'd be happy to make do with half a loaf of white bread and a Coca-Cola, same as the natives eat — given half a chance."

Of course, Charity knew how we felt. But then, as she said to me: "The Kingdom of God is not meat and drink, Harry. So Paul said to the Romans before he went out and killed the *tsotsis* and skellums."

Once a month, on average, she was called home to the sick and dying in her family. For the rest, she left the house only on Sundays for Church, dressed in a long white robe, cape and staff, decorated with blue moons and stars, a silver star of David on a green ribbon pinned to her breast. Otherwise she never went on the street.

"There are *tsotsis* and skellums in the street. I pray God the police will kill them. They are bad natives."

"What about the bad white people?"

She looked surprised. "God himself will kill them."

Faced by her, Wyner — who actually read the stuff — quoted Roy Campbell. She showed, he said, "the sullen dignity of beaten tribes."

I say balls. She was simply a sour old bitch. Come to think of it she used to refer to Jan Smuts as Baas Smuts and to Dr Malan as Big Baas Malan. How's that for a sense of priorities? I knew plenty of white nazis. I mean, looking no further than the guys who came over from Germany at the end of the war you could make up an entire rugby team — picking only the guys who looked like Martin Bormann. Charity, however, was my first black fascist.

3

"There are confounded blackguards amongst us," Brother Donally regularly announced, cleaning the board with great swishing circles, the words exploding over his head in little puffs of chalk dust.

What a yawn it was when he went on like that.

"Bad eggs, boys from rough surroundings who, although we are in September already and face the rigours of a matric examination in just six weeks' time, give to all the world the impression that this formidable obstacle lies behind them. To be sure, hearing their raving chatter the Saints themselves would be believing they'd already faced the stern Judge and been ushered into paradise with full marks. Whereas . . . beneath their toes the pit gapes."

He cleaned the board so fast his cassock sleeves snapped and spat around his wrists. He had been showing us the workings of the Shakespearian pentameter in lines from *Macbeth*. The room was very hot. Hardly anybody knew how to spell Shakespeare never mind *scan* him. I mean, I *ask* you. Jeez! Anyway, he'd pulled the lines to bits as if he were off on a bayonet charge, counting the syllables with sergeant major's yelps, flashing at the iambs and zonking the feet with a thudding forefinger on the black steel surface of the board.

Total stupefaction. Total, but for the front row of course, altar servers to a man, class toadies. To say their name, tongue against roof of the mouth, air sucked in sharply until your saliva rattles behind the back teeth . . . SCHHH-LOEPS! Life members of the Sodality of Mary, Founder Squires of da Gama, Brothers of the Third Order of St Francis, those lovers of lambs and budgie kissers, pockets stuffed with rosary beads, miraculous medals on chains, chests strapped into scapulas tighter than the foot bindings of Japanese women; hit-men for the Catholic Mothers' League, guys who wore bicycle clips and didn't care who knew it, who slavered to clean the board duster . . . when they weren't polishing their haloes.

These provided Donally's solid centre of support, clapped all his jokes and were always ready with the astonished gasp — "Gosh, Brother!" — when he said something incredibly obvious. These guys waved to each other when they passed like popes, one and a half fingers waggled in front of the chest: more a blessing than a wave, really. Hoendervoegt, who collected indulgences, claimed to have wiped off all his fire time in purgatory with a couple of good plenaries early on and then stacked up the temporals until he reckoned he was nine thousand years into the black just in case; Langenegger, who prayed for the stigmata and turned up one day with a hole in his left palm and claimed it was beginning — but then the wound went septic and it turned out his brother had stabbed him there with an apple corer; Gebhardt the German, only guy who could have checked Shuckel's story that he had read Karl Marx in the original, and burst into tears when we asked him to do so, refused because he said communism was a mortal sin. Gebhardt was horribly in love with plump little Mother Imelda who took the convent girls for hockey; and, of course, Smees with the bad breath, Gebhardt's rival in love, who had a vision of the Virgin Mary standing on a cloud. She appeared to him in the darkroom and stayed only a few seconds, but considering the small size of that room and Smees's breath you couldn't blame her. After the experience he attempted to join the Children of Mary. He was acting on instructions, he said, and he bought a white mantilla to wear to Mass. But the Children took girls only and so Smees wrote a letter to the Pope asking special permission. He was still waiting. And, of course, then there was the archangel of them all, the only guy I've known who from the time he was seven wanted to be a saint when he grew up — viz Kenny "Mother's Little" Darling. Once, Jack Wyner had sat with the schloeps but when he came over to us, instead of taking a seat at the back, he'd slipped back half-way down the class. Always hedging his bets was old Wyner.

All the expression in Donally's face took place below his

eyebrows. He'd stamp and flap and make hideous faces — the famous "Chinese dragon", the "incredible Witchdoctor" and so on. But they never reached up to his forehead which curved, above his eyes, dead white and still as a saucer, owing, I suppose, to the steel plate the surgeons had laid between skin and skull when he got whatever wound it had been in whichever war. Sometimes, on a really hot afternoon when he went into his soul on the rack routine, the movement of him, a big man inside a bigger cassock, got a breeze up around the head of the class. Those of us further back sweltered in summer and suffocated in winter with the radiators turned up to broil. When the holy guys up front wanted to be really mean, on a signal from Smees they had this trick of farting in unison, and what with old Donally flapping like the north wind and wafting it down the class it was sheer murder. He never allowed the windows to be opened. "Something might fly in," he explained with a cruel smile, staring hard behind his thick glasses, always coated with chalk dust, his eyes wandering in different directions.

"The bad eggs to which I'm referring, not a thousand miles away from this classroom, stink to high heaven. Only God in his mercy can save them from a rotten end. If indeed he has not turned his face. However, I am after seeing them very, very clearly."

One eye fixed on me while the other went in search of a second victim, completing a circuit of the class before coming to rest on van Dam, directly behind me. He was close up to my left ear giving me a long story in excited, warm pants:

". . . now when you get this Trudy, only thirteen remember, Harry, not that we're superstitious — right? You grab her, right? And then you don't french-kiss her. That's *nothing*. No! Get hold of her neck and kiss around there for a while. Work your way up.

"Get to an ear . . . O.K? You listening, Harry? Right, so the lobe first, a few nibbles on the lobe, gently, take your time and THEN — zip! You push your tongue deep down into her ear. This is the bit you got to watch out for. She'll . . . go . . . CRAZY! Have you on the floor before you know it, panties around her knees, absolutely BEGGING for it . . ."

Donally came down the aisle and leaned above us like a

stricken bluegum. "Now what would a boy who knows nothing be saying to a boy who knows next to nothing?" he asked van Dam in the calm tones which were always a bad sign. He lost his temper, you see, often, and would shout and spit and throw things. I don't think he liked giving way to these rages. Maybe they carried him back to the dreadful wars. In Ireland, they said, he once nearly killed a boy by flinging him into the blackboard. For that he was sent, as a reward Shuckel maintained, to South Africa by his canny bosses back in old Eire who knew a thing or two about the colonial blackguardly boy. I mean, he broke a board ruler of heavy seasoned pine across Yannovitch's shoulder once and he wasn't even trying.

"Nothing, Brother," van Dam said meekly.

Donally's flat hand got van Dam between the shoulder blades with a deep boom.

"Notice," Donally said, "the old truth illustrated: empty vessels make the most noise."

The front row threw themselves about at this sally and van Dam collapsed in a winded sort of a way gagging a bit which (thank God) seemed to mollify Donally. A strong smell of brandy and tobacco drifted from his cassock whose dull black was giving way to the worn brown shine of age with greasy, frayed sleeve-ends out of which thick square wrists protruded, black with hair where the chalk dust stuck like pollen and rested like dandruff on his shoulders. Everything about him was rough and violent except his forehead. Seen from below it had the cold curve of a lavatory bowl. I expected the usual assault. The old whapping blows flat-handed on the back of the skull, driving my nose towards the dried-up inkwell. I was saved by the bell which rang for the *Angelus*, and we stood up to pray:

The Angel of the Lord declared unto Mary . . .

Our prayers were aimed at the statue of the Virgin standing on a wall bracket about four foot up in the corner of the classroom. *Regina Coeli*. Queen of Heaven . . . A candle flickered in a red jar before her bare toes. She stood on the globe of the world with a little green snake wriggling beneath her bare feet, its head showing under her right heel, tongue forked. A bit like Gina Lollobrigida, Our Lady looked. Only thinner. With a lot of red to her high cheek bones. Lovely olive skin. The blue and white of her gown had faded over the years. Held up by a thin wire a couple of inches above her head was a brass circlet, her crown of stars, drooping a bit over one eye like a schoolboy's boater, giving her a rakish look. Her nose had been struck cleanly off by the board duster flung at somebody Brother Donally had marked for death and missed. It had been glued back on rather carelessly and when you looked at her in three-quarter profile her nose had a beautiful curve. You might have said that board duster put an end to her Italian virginity and made her a Jewish momma again. Which was only fair, when you think about it.

We prayed on the hour throughout the day, always the "Hail Mary" and at twelve o'clock, the *Angelus*. The "Hail Mary" took just two deep breaths. One for the brisk run-up through the salutation: only key words pronounced in full: *Hail Mary fngngngngngrace the Lordingngng thee blessedartngngngngngst women angngngngngofthywombJesus* . . . and then a quick breather teetering on the summit, and the downhill race through the invocation to see who finished first: *Holy Maryrhgngn gnGodprayforussinnersnowangngngourdeathAmen.*

Besides Catholics, St Bonaventure's took in Jews, Protestants and Mohammedans from the Diplomatic Corps; grabbed anybody, in fact, who could cough up the fees. It was a status thing really. Ours was the only private English school for miles around. Non-Catholics staggered to their feet on the hour for prayers same as everyone else, only they didn't have to say anything. Just stood there swaying, kind of glassy-eyed, picking their noses maybe. Safety in numbers. Protestants were there to pay and to ride shotgun. It was Indian country. We Catholics, huddled together for warmth, you might have said, packed in over an area of about ten rugby fields. Our territory was the Parish Church of the Community of the Resurrection and the Convent of Our Lady of Sorrows (divided from our playground only by a battered hedge). We being St Bonaventure's College for Boys, run by the brothers of the saint's holy order, plus subsidiary buildings — the Scout and School and Parish Halls, Brothers' House, Nunnery, Priest's House, pumphouse, cricket pavilion, tennis courts, swimming pool, cadet armoury and playing fields tightly packed, lumped even, slap-bang in the middle of a suburb — (what am I saying?) in the middle of a whole damn world — crammed to the eyeballs with red hot fanatical Afrikaners, great hairy Calvinists, the short back and sides brigade, black suits and shiny boots and bibles bigger than tombstones. When these guys finished with kaffirs for breakfast it was Catholics they turned to for afters. And the next worse thing to letting your daughter marry a kaffir was to find a Roman in your woodshed. Come to think of it the school with its high fences, tall cast-iron gates, huge white walls, stone windows and acres of red verandahs had the feeling of a medieval hospice. It looked the sort of place they put you into if you showed the dreaded buboes and started breathing strangely. Once inside the great gates slammed behind you. Around the walls the Dragon of Geneva roamed daring the Whore of Rome to come out and fight.

The Calvinists wanted us out. Trouble was that there had been Romans in the woodshed before the Puritans bought the garden. Fresh-faced out from Eire half a century before the Brothers of St Bonaventure had bought the ground from the local chief with a couple of bags of blarney and, so the story went, the promise of a fat nun or two, and raised the Pope's banner in the shale.

If the Dragon didn't get much devouring done, it huffed and puffed things pretty hot for the Papists. First of all the government cut off all state money. The Fathers of the Resurrection responded by soaking the richer parishioners. College and Convent promptly doubled their fees. The PTA organised Bring and Buys and Cake and Candy Sales. They collected jumble and raffled tins of Spam and managed for a while. The line held. The Dragon changed its tactics. It began jingling its small change. Church, school and convent took one look at the money offered for the smallest parcels of land, a tennis court here, a chapel there, the playing field toilets, and fell even as they were tempted. All the time I was at St Bonaventure's there was less of it. It was like living on a sandbar with a gentle tide coming in. So quiet and slow that you didn't realise that bit by bit the ground you stood on was washing away under your feet.

And the Word was made Flesh and dwelt amongst Us . . .

The class genuflected heavily in the aisles between the

40

desks. Felix Greenbaum prayed with clasped hands through a blocked nose: the only chap who knew all the prayers by heart plus the Litany. After years of practice most of us still needed help, even the schloeps. Not Greenbaum.

Oddly enough, I heard that he wasn't much thought of at *schul*, old Greenbaum. Just goes to show. Unhappy sort of guy, poor Felix. His big brother was a class golfer, friends with Bobby Locke, and Greenbaum wanted to be like his big brother. Only he was not good with a ball. I'd see him in a corner of the playground at break, away in a corner, with an old hockey stick and a pine cone, practising his putting. He'd a bad habit of dropping his chin undoubtedly developed over years of leading the prayers:

> Hail Holy Bary, Bother of Bercy, Hail, Our sweetness,
> light and hobe . . .

Greenbaum intoned, eyes shut. Brother Donally stood directly beneath the statue of the Virgin. She stared blindly down her broken nose at his untroubled forehead.

The bell went for the lunch break. Donally got me as I was passing his desk. Yannovitch and van Dam lingered pointedly to show that they would give me moral support, but he waved them out with a grim little smile.

"Don't let me keep you from your lunch gentlemen. Mr Moto and I are after having a little word in private."

He settled back in his desk and I kind of shifted around in front of him wondering where to look. He didn't have that problem because he could let his eyes wander. When he reckoned I'd had enough of the silent treatment he fought a brief battle to get both eyes to focus on me, soon gave up and allowed one eye to wander off and look out of the window where the white, flat clouds passed sluggishly. He was upset, white at the lips and breathing through his nose with a choked whistle, wet and piercing with the tone and range of a plastic bird warbler filled with water.

"Young fool. You'll grease the halter yet, Moto. By all means go to hell your own way then — but first get your matric. For the sake of your old Mom and Dad who've skimped and saved to give you a good Catholic education. Costs a penny it does. I'm sure your father — though we've not had the pleasure of acquaintance — I'll be bound he isn't nipping down to the local and sozzling away the housekeeping, or throwing it after the dogs of a Saturday night. You're a lucky boy. Some I could name don't give *that* for the children God gave 'em. Wife beaters! Poor men in the sway of the Gombeens!'' He snapped his fingers like twigs breaking. "And if that doesn't touch you then think of your last hours. Even if you live to be eighty. It may seem a long while now with no more than sixteen at your back, but they'll go like a flash, believe me, and we'll have you on your death bed quick as a wink.'' He clapped me on the shoulders and fell back on his chair contentedly: "Ah, you've taken the first step, the loose companions in the back row, next will come the hashish in the toilet during big break, then the loose girls in the dark. And before long you'll be thinking yourself a power in the land. But remember, Moto, the wages of sin . . . Remember, there are always accidents to interrupt a man. Think of your close shave with the mercury vapour. Next breath might have been your last. Snuffed at sixteen. Would you be thinking that a long life? How long is eternity?''

I envied him his vision of the wickedness of things. Where in God's name *were* these bad eggs, gambling and pissing it up and going to the dogs? As for wife beating . . . you had only to look at the mothers sailing through the school gates each day in their Lincoln Continentals, Baby Jags or Mercedes Coupes, hair permed like Nazi helmets, freshly lit Rothmans dangling from the lower lip, box of fifty on their laps, and the big muscles developed on the driving range four afternoons a week flexing nicely in their forearms as they worked the steering wheel, to see the silliness of that. Once in a while somebody would step out of line. True. Brother Heaney's nerve broke in '57 and he ran away. It was hushed up. They said he had gone on an indefinite retreat somewhere in the Lowveld and Brother Donally did a whitewashing job, raging on for weeks about this "brave move back to the simple life of the Desert Fathers.'' Then, there was Old Brother Conally who was supposed to have the hots for Smees's old lady, a plump red-head who could be seen parked at the fence in her Oldsmobile convertible when he was coaching the under-thirteen cricket team, with her servant girl in the back, acting as a kind of chaperone, I suppose. But since he never did more than wander over and lean up against her driving mirror and mop his face a lot while they talked you could hardly call it a grand passion. Granted it was rumoured that Brother O'Leary wanted to become a homeopath. Some guys who'd been invited to his room in the Brothers' House said that he asked them to spit into the pans on a little scale. Afterwards he gave out biscuits and made them promise to be in touch if ever they got cancer. But that was about the size of it. Occasional deaths among the brothers broke the tedium. A welcome surprise because it meant a half-holiday, but not to be relied upon.

Nearer home the truth was, if anything, even further away from Donally's view of the wickedness of things. Try as I did I simply could not imagine my old man heading out on Saturday nights for his "local". My father with his single brandy and water after work, measured from the liquor cabinet standing in the corner of the lounge, always kept tightly locked in case "the servants" (servants always suddenly got into the plural when booze was mentioned) "helped themselves". I saw my father delving and clinking among the mirrors lining the insides of the cabinet, like a priest fiddling among the curtains of the tabernacle to pull out his little glass chalice and its tot of *Oudemeester*. And anyway, our "local" simply wasn't something down to which you could "nip" — ho, ho! It was a ten-minute drive presuming you went to the nearest bar, The Oxwagon, a low, brown, concrete bunker with little frosted windows and a small red verandah smelling of stale beer and vomit. The flower beds built of a scratchy purple brick that sandpapered the skin off your calves if you got too close, stood like coffins showing a few delphiniums choking in cigarette ash and matchsticks. As for going to the dogs — who'd ever seen a greyhound except on the films? Racing them was illegal anyway. It wasn't that Donally made these things up. I could have forgiven him that. No, what was so sad was that the sorts of dangerous living Donally pictured did happen, but they happened elsewhere. Everything always happened elsewhere. That was the trouble. That was the whole bloody trouble.

The door of the classroom opened very slowly and the cleaner entered on his knees. He wanted to sweep up and clear the lunch papers. He stopped when he saw us with just his head around the door. "Come in, John," Donally ordered . . .

The man stayed put. "Maybe his name isn't John, Brother."

"They're all called John," Donally said.

He glared at me. "Depart from me ye cursed — "

As I went I saw the cleaner crawling among the desks. In his khaki shorts and tunic he blended with the desks. I mean, you had to look twice.

Cleaners, groundsmen, gardeners, you always had to look twice to see them. The school was kept going by a whole army of invisible black people who lived in a long barracks behind the cricket pavilion. They were there and yet they were not there. They had to appear in front of your nose to be noticed. As with visions, one had to be alone to see them: a shadow on the marble wall of the urinal; the khaki shirt flapping like a tent polishing the copper fittings; or overhead a bundle of rags suspended from the ceiling, cleaning the fanlight. If I stared they would stop and make a point of waiting until I looked away. After a while the implications of this dawned on me. They saw me before I spotted them, slithering like crabs at the far ends of the enormous red verandahs, crouching over brush and polish tin, or like nesting birds peering from the roof gutters, black bedraggled birds perching with specially formed flannel beaks on tall ladders, busy at the assembly hall windows, shining tiny sections of glass one pane a day, or like deformed beggars waiting on the other side of every door, backing away and hideously apologetic, clutching cans of Brasso and yellow dusters, or like crippled veterans of wars we knew nothing of leaning on their brooms and turning to watch as I climbed the narrow flights of stairs to my classroom. Trouble was once I'd begun to notice them, I couldn't stop. They were everywhere.

Shuckel, van Dam and Yannovitch were waiting for me on the playground, at the fence alongside the main road. Van Dam was obviously terrified. He kept plucking at the seat of his pants.

"What's the matter?" I said.

"Indian hit him there with a tomahawk," Shuckel answered.

"Damn seam gets stuck in the crack. Jeez man, you were

44

in there a long time. What'd old Donally want?"

The playground was a sun-baked square of red sand and shale with balding, skinny fir trees around the edges. There was a fight on. Two boys began hitting and kicking each other. They fell on the ground and a crowd began to gather, eating sandwiches, sipping Cokes. Whenever one of the figures rolled out of the circle some chap would carefully push him back into the middle of the ring with his toe. I pointed them out to Yannovitch.

"As a prefect, I thought it was your job to stop fights on the playground?"

He turned away. "Oh, it's them: Wilcox and Nasser. They can kill each other. Who cares? They're always at it. Shuckel says that they're homos and this is the only way they can meet."

"For God's sake, Moto!" van Dam shouted, scratching away at his backside worse than ever. "What did he say?"

"We talked about Trudy, actually. Remember you were telling me about her? As randy as hell, old Trudy. It was all your fault I got bawled out. So when Donally asked me to explain I looked him straight in the eye. It's Trudy, I said, at the convent, Brother. Only thirteen, but get your tongue in her ear her pants pop off. Van Dam says so, Brother."

"Oh Jeez! Come on . . . you're chaffing me, Moto. Hey? I don't believe you. I mean you wouldn't say *that*."

"Fantastic stuff!" Shuckel applauded. "What did he say then?"

"Well, you know how he is about sex?" I waved them closer. Van Dam closed his eyes. "He looked at me for a long time. First with one eye and then the other. Then he leans across the desk and he whispers: 'Moto, me lad, which ear were you saying it was?'" When they'd stopped laughing Yannovitch looked hard at me and shook his head. "He's after you, Harry. He's got you lined up in his sights and if he can get his eyes together he'll pick you off."

"But dammit, why should he bother? He's convinced I'm finished anyway. If a man jumps off a skyscraper why bother to give him a shove as he passes your window?"

"Better be safe than sorry," Yannovitch said.

Going back to the classroom when the bell rang who should I bump into coming around the corner but the cleaner with his broom, bucket and sack of lunch papers. He dropped everything and followed it down, changing in a trice into a kind of drunken octopus scrabbling at the feet of the passing boys for the scattering papers. He had trouble because every so often a couple of jokers would dribble a ball of paper around the corridor shouting, "Hey, hey, pass it here — out to the wing, man!" I picked up his broom and bucket.

"Tell me something," I said, "truly now — what *is* your name?"

Still on his hands and knees he stared up at me, surprised first, then frightened, then finally angry. "It's John, baas. My name is John." I began to understand then that not only were they everywhere, but they were all called John. And they weren't planning to break cover just yet.

4

On Wednesday afternoon Jack Wyner was otherwise engaged. There was no swimming and we faced the problem of deciding what to do. The reason for Wyner being otherwise engaged was his weekly altar servers' meeting. There were masses of altar boys and these get-togethers were known as the Nuremberg rallies. His membership was a hangover from his toadie days before he became a bad egg. He resigned from his other clubs when he came over to us: the Society of St Vincent de Paul, the Sodality of Mary, the choir, Squires of da Gama, Young Stigmatists, Volunteer Carpenters for Christ and so on. But the altar servers were like the Mafia. They never let go.

Always willing to help a friend we tried to get him expelled. Yannovitch had him nick a couple of packets of communion wafers and some wine from the Sacristy before serving early morning Mass. Eager to oblige, I'll say that for him, old Wyner outdid himself and lifted about three weeks' supply of the stuff and met us behind the parish hall, beaming away. We drank the wine at one sitting. It was pretty lousy, sweet and heavy, made in Israel, with a blue star of David on the label but it helped to wash down the wafers which tasted like cardboard. Van Dam annoyed everybody by acting big, holding the bottle up to the light between swigs, rolling it around on his tongue and spitting it onto the grass saying things like, "Ah Vatican '99, I see. A motherly little wine, superior but cloistered and rather nunnish on the tongue . . ." Unfortunately the theft was never discovered mainly, I suspect, because Brother Emmanuel, the Sacristan, liked his tipple and probably thought he'd sunk the booze himself. Even so, having got Wyner to steal the wine we couldn't leave it at that and live with our failure.

Shuckel came up with an idea for getting us off the hook. We had this free period in class when we bored ourselves silly compiling dossiers of information on subjects of our choice: Yannovitch was busy dredging up the history of Afrikaner Nationalists who had passed up the Second World War in order to stay home and blow up bridges and afterwards got to be big-shots in the Government. Van Dam wrote stories for television, which he said his brother who knew somebody incredibly powerful in the Union Buildings in Pretoria had told him was definitely coming in 1962 and he wanted to be ready; Jack Wyner collected stamps (he would); and Shuckel stuck into a green cardboard folder the pictures of known acquaintances of Karl Marx just to keep everybody guessing, he said, until the last day when he would shove in the man himself and scare the living shits out of old Donally. Casually, he borrowed Wyner's stamp album just before Donally made his weekly collection to pick over the rubbish, telling Jack that he wanted to check his Russian section and carefully entered an entire set of sacramental hosts under the section for Mauritius — using corners and all.

Wyner didn't have a leg to stand on. The Altar Servers' Soviet sent for him. I gather they didn't hit him, just frightened him a bit by pointing out that what he had taken was no ordinary loot, but the sacred materials awaiting transubstantiation during the Consecration of the Mass into the sacred body and blood of our Lord Jesus Christ, that he'd missed (if he had missed) committing sacrilege by inches, was almost certainly in a state of mortal sin and if he died that instant would roast in hell for all eternity.

With all that brimstone up his nostrils poor Jack sang like a canary. But the stout chap never fingered us. Amazingly, the Klan didn't expel him. Which goes to show, I suppose, that God's mercy is infinite, or, as is more likely, there was no sin so black the Altar Servers could not countenance it for the sake of solidarity.

On Wednesday afternoons we rode to Big Lou Abramowitz's shop for fish and chips, out towards Queen Mary Location along Piet Retief Avenue, a main road howling with heavy traffic, carrying battered third-class taxis and racketing kikuyu-green buses jammed to the eyeballs with blacks from the Location. The buses were called Green Mambas, I think because they appeared from nowhere and hit you without warning. And hundreds of cars. We had to watch for those. You had the impression that applicants on taking their licence swore to kill at least one cyclist before hanging up the old driving gloves. What could you expect, van Dam demanded: guys on bikes deserved it. If you were anywhere near decent you'd be driving a car.

Lou's was the last in a line of single-storied, flat-roofed little shops: bicycles, groceries, dry-cleaning, pants & vests, bottle store, fish and chips. The Van Riebeeckshof Shopping Centre it was called. That's putting it grandly. The shops floated on a raft of grey concrete set well back from the road, alongside which the pavement of hard-baked sand littered with stones, uneven as a dried river bed, flowed in its abundant red dust carrying scraps of yellowing newspaper, dried and stiffened by the sun, the *Golden City Post* and the *Sunday Times* once used to wrap fish and chips and still showing grease stains and patches of encrusted salt. Rich litter of a life we never had but strangely yearned for: pint milk cartons, their waxen sides gleaming, with the Bolvrede Dairy's lettering showing through the furred dust, faintly blue like veins; bus tickets; empty cigarette packets, little ones, in cheap biscuit and indigo wrappers without cellophane: Venus and Five Star, good brands to buy because they came in fives; brandy, vodka, gin, and cane-spirit bottles, split whole from their thick, uneven bases, filling with sand, half-jacks and the little quarter-size bottles known as five-bob nips. We bought the same when there was a party because they decanted nicely into hip-flasks.

We parked our bikes against the window where a painted fish was standing on its tail, six foot high, its flesh grey, scales black. One eye stared helplessly at the world. Across its gill was lettered in flaking blue, THE MILKY WAY TEA ROOM. A broad red Coca-Cola band sealed the top of the window which was covered with a heavy duty wire mesh screen. The tail of the Y in WAY had been pulled back in a thickening line until it reached the M in MILKY where it grew a rocket nose set about with tiny stars and half a moon. Wavy streaks trailing behind gave the speed of the craft and the thrust of its engines. The window was decorated with a pyramid of dusty vinegar bottles and a sprinkling of dead flies.

A wall of wire mesh about eight foot high divided the shop and the marble counter with its separate supplies of salt, vinegar and sheets of newspaper. Whites got their chips in the *Times* and Blacks in the *Post*. On the white counter was the cash till and on a shelf above it, very prominent, Lou's service pistol. Lou was busy at the frying stove bending to the baths of oil, shaking chip baskets and slapping pieces of floury fish with a flick of the wrist in the enamel batter-pans. A queue of Blacks stretched back to the door. The White section was empty.

"Be with you boys in half a mo." Lou smiled sideways. An old white apron around his middle strained in tight grooves where his belly fought clear of it and rolled over the edge. A tall guy, old Lou, six six, maybe, in his socks, with a big square chest set a step back from his gut like the top of a sideboard and hairy, I mean really *matted*, the hairs poking through his rayon see-through shirt and this big head, purple as an aubergine. You might not like old Lou's politics, as Shuckel was fond of saying, but you simply *had* to look up to him. You're telling me — in the way you looked up to King Kong.

Lou flipped a basketful of hot chips onto a piece of newspaper and turned to the customer, a huge guy with bigger muscles in his neck than I had in my calves. "Salt 'n' vinegar?" Lou paused with his hand on the can of salt. The man nodded. Without taking his hand off the salt can Lou reached over and pulled the man half-way over the counter. "Yes?" He shook him like a rag doll and released him so he slammed into the woman behind him. The queue giggled and swayed like a Chinese dragon as the shock passed down the line. The customer's chin kind of folded over his Adam's apple and he kept his eyes on the ground. "Remember your manners," Lou told the queue over his lowered head, "you're not in the bloody jungle. Now, we'll try again shall we?" He lifted the tin shaker, "Salt?"

"Yes, my baas."

Lou soused the chips with vinegar and wrapped the parcel with quick little folds, tucks and a final pat. "Sixpence." He stuck out a hand like a palm leaf. "You know, my boy, you don't want fish and chips, you should be eating monkey-nuts and swinging from trees." He backed away to the cash till, taking his pistol from the shelf before opening the cash drawer. The waiting crowd fell about at this sally. Lou's sense of humour evidently appealed greatly, which was something that had always struck me as rather odd, especially since he made no secret of his hatred for Africans. He told us quite openly that he expected one of them to murder him. That was why he kept the gun very much in evidence. He pointed to the number of would-be assassins he'd shot — three in all — as proof of the fact that it was only a matter of time. But he planned, he said, as was only right and proper, to take plenty more with him before he went. They'd have to get up very early in the morning to polish off old Lou. Here he turned to the crowd and brandished his pistol. "Until then you bloody well behave yourselves, you black baboons!"

The queue rocked delightedly and looking at them I wondered whether amongst the smiling faces was the man who would one day get up early enough to do in Lou Abramowitz.

On Wednesday afternoons we ate Lou's chips, so hot they burnt the fingers, sitting on the concrete steps of the Van Riebeeckshof Shopping Centre. It was the last stop before the African Location. Barefoot kids kicked tin cans about, tatty khaki shorts flapping at their bony knees; others, very smart and correct in school caps, ties and shiny black toe-capped shoes, held their mother's hands looking eerily subdued. Women balanced on their heads cardboard boxes tied with string, tins of paraffin, black or yellow suitcases, scratched tin trunks clanking with padlocks and plastered with stickers of faraway towns: Hammanskraal, Rustenburg, Pietersburg. Clutching string bags thicker than fishnets, old washgirls, all gummy smiles and marble forearm muscles, counted their change carefully from pink palms into black leather zip purses. Fat, cheeky young tarts with yellow and purple berets dipping over their eyes, in tight short skirts strapped around their buttocks and grubby men's shirts missing buttons that showed their breasts bounding, jived with each other to the rock'n'roll and kwela music pounding out of the speakers above the bicycle shop. Grander women dressed to kill in high heels and fishnet nylons stared out at the world from behind the veils of their rakish little hats; they wore dark beauty spots on their cheekbones and fire-red lipstick glowing on their pallid, bleached faces. Houseboys, garden boys, skinny legged flat-boys, knock-knees circled by the green or red or blue piping of their baggy shorts threw dice. Fancy crooks in lightweight summer suits, brown and white golf shoes carrying pigskin briefcases casually held by just the corner between two fingers and six differently coloured ball-point pens clipped in the breast pocket chatted with other natty dressers — off-duty cooks or clerks or ponces perhaps, in dark Barathea blazers, silver-grey pants with knife-edge creases and carefully brushed brown suedes, who tapped their 'Nulook' Gloria Sunshine sunglasses on their noses with assured fingers, twirling their umbrellas and mopping their brows with silken handkerchiefs. Leaning up against the sections of wall that caught a little shade, old men tilted their heads to catch the last dribbles of sweet sherry from the necks of half-jacks, while ragged kids chased each other jumping over their legs. We joined the long line of diners on the edge of the concrete strip which ran the length of the shopping centre, red dust lapping our feet, wolfing fish and chips washed down with swigs from family-sized bottles of Coke or cartons of milk.

Say what you like, the place looked good. And I knew why. It was simply being among all these different people coming and going and *mixing* in a small place, waiting between buses, slapping the bottom of the Coke bottle, wiping the salt, vinegar and cooking oil from the newspaper with a crust of bread and licking your fingers. It wasn't much but it was something. Something on the go.

On Wednesday afternoons, in their grey-pleated hockey skirts, the convent girls went scudding across the sandy playing field, which was hidden behind a thick hedge polka-dotted with red berries reputedly poisonous and wicked little thorns. Being the only Catholic girls' school this side of the Magaliesberg there was no one to play with them and so they picked up teams amongst themselves. On Wednesday afternoons, Mother Imelda tucked up her habit into a pair of thick khaki socks and pumped up and down the touchline stopping now and then to shake the spit from her whistle.

When I arrived that small-time visionary Arthur Smees was

standing at the one gap in the hedge that gave a clear view of the field. He was literally drooling at the poetry of Mother Imelda's soft khaki calves as she sped up and down the field. I got ready to ignore him. Next door, on the tarmac tennis courts, little plump girls hopping with elbows bent held racquets above their heads like traffic cops halting traffic, gently pushing tennis balls across the sagging nets with a soft bass note of the strings.

Smees sidled over. "Hullo Harry. Who've you come to see? Betcha I know — it's Mary Smithson, what's the bet? You be careful. She's Trevor Goble's girl. He'll kill you, if he finds out."

"Get stuffed, Arthur."

I saw Mary. She was sweeping the ball wildly, missed and coming up with her back swing, hit Mina in the face and made her collide with Dottie, who was reaching her stick for the ball with fierce concentration. Dottie tumbled awkwardly in the sand and grimaced as she surfaced, holding her right wrist. Mother Imelda gave a blast on her whistle and waved her arms. The game stopped.

"Something tells me Mother Imelda's spotted you, Arthur. Look, she's playing to the gallery — for Christ's sake!"

"Don't take the name of the Lord in vain."

"Listen to who is talking! Who's been taking liberties with His old lady in the darkroom? Seen any good visions lately, Arthur?"

"You've got a filthy mind." His eyes watered. "By the way, I hear you can't get an Identity Card. What does it mean, I wonder?"

I pursed my lips. "Kiss me and find out. If you're arrested, I'm a Coloured. O.K.?"

"You're disgusting, Moto."

On Wednesday afternoons even in hockey socks her legs were wonderful, curving under the heavy blue wool. Her kneecaps were egg-smooth where the short grey-pleated skirt ended. Agreed, she was a bit beanpole-ish. But stretches of her were fantastically beautiful. Her belly pushing against her waistband made a surprising curve, hip to hip. Her breasts were small. They barely lifted her shirt. Bee stings, Yannovitch called them. But they were bigger than mine so who was I to complain? The V-neck of her open shirt was sandy with tiny freckles. Behind her head, caught in a green rubber band, her pony tail, swinging with the light behind it showed on one side then the other the wispy down on her neck where her hairline ended. Sideways, I saw the same wispiness along her upper lip, trapping a tiny drop of sweat just left of a nostril. Her cheeks were pink and her lips white from running. She walked towards me bouncing her scuffed hockey stick with its dangling black cotton binding off the toe of her black canvas boots sending little spurts of dust out of the laces. Though put off by the presence of Smees I had to act quickly, before the others came. I blurted out my invitation to the dance and she said yes, just like that, and I fell off my bicycle. We were both laughing when Mina arrived with her stretcher party. Dottie was white-faced, stockings around her ankles, showing Coke-bottle calves. She managed a tearful smile. Mother Imelda looked at me as if she'd discovered King Farouk among her novices.

"You've got a filthy laugh, Harry Moto," Mina spoke through the hankie.

"Sorry about your mouth, Min." Mary gave her a hug.

"Come Mary," Mother Imelda commanded, "let us help this poor girl inside."

As they bore her away Mina turned and looked straight at my fly. She stared so hard that for a dreadful moment I thought I must have come adrift again. I glanced down. Mina removed the hankie and smiled. "Choof, choof, choof!" she mouthed triumphantly. Her split lip had been bleeding on her teeth.

Smees heard me ask Mary to the dance. I knew that because of what happened later.

On Wednesday afternoons we sometimes went to Koelietown. A place apart and strictly out of bounds and the closest we would ever get, we told ourselves, to going abroad. If it had not been for Koelietown I think we would have believed like everyone else in the three principal things: that the earth was flat; that we were put on it to die of boredom; that anyone attempting to escape would fall off the edge. Koelietown was crammed into a corner of the city, an odd triangle, a rough diamond with its southern base hard against the railway shunting yards, blocked on the west by the great marshalling sheds and on the east hemmed in by the old town cemetery, a wild stony place of overgrown yew trees, its dead forgotten under trim coverings of green gravel; only in its northern narrows did Koelietown run relatively free, pushing a dirty snub nose into the white city centre a few blocks left of the Central Police Station on busy Main Street where the traffic moved nose to tail all day and at night nothing moved at all. In Koelietown the living were packed in like the dead in the old cemetery next door, crowded into the tawdry half-mile above and below their shops, in doorways, on rooftops, squatting in alleyways or sleeping on the pavements which the black whores patrolled in the evenings with purple-ringed eyes and oily black wigs and a slow, dragging walk on bandaged ankles, on the look-out for patrolling cop vans as they touted for customers, usually white toughs who came cruising, an arm stuck out of the window, shirtsleeves rolled up to the armpit to show off the muscle bulging over the door of Chev or Buick, all flashing fintails and brake-lights like pools of blood. Shopkeepers bawled their wares outside shop windows blazing with promises of perpetual sales, eternal credit and no deposit. Hashish from a doorway, joss fumes in a window, cachous, new leather, curry, chapattis and the honeyed offers of something for nothing: *A Third Off for Cash! And One Suit Free!* and *Two Pounds Down! And Two Pants Free!* and *Fifty-Two Weeks to Pay! And Five Shirts Free!* -- old sweat, gusts of hot air from the eating houses where nightwatchmen off-duty from the smart shops in the city centre, in khaki greatcoats and peaked caps, sat at dawn dunking handfuls of stiff porridge in a little gravy, leaning on their heavy knobkerries, staring through the steamy windows, while in the doorways of the little crammed cafes stern washerwomen humping babies and black bags jostled nervous young houseboys hand in hand buying samoosas, cold, yellow, greasy, brittle triangles, or purple doughnuts sprinkled with coconut, leaking jam, black as octopus ink. Proud white madams in silver-thread slack-suits, dripping diamonds, under beehives so high and real that you expected furious black swarms to come zinging out of their ears at any moment, shifted off tartan car-seats, kneed open the doors of baby Jags and powder-blue Mercs, locked their handbags fiercely into their armpits and headed for the SALES! Little old grannies made the long journey from the kraal dragging along spindly children with lumps on their heads for consultations with the muti-man and he took them for half a year's wages and gave them bat's penis and dried roots in a little leather bag. Fake Indian doctors with more letters after their names than company directors, sold bracelets, copper against arthritis, elephant hair for luck, to jolly housewives, and ground gemsbok horn, Spanish fly and French letters, some multicoloured, some horned and fretted, some with funny faces, to blushing schoolboys. Cocky young guys, one eye hidden under a rakish white beret, sidled up on street corners and in urgent whispers offered solid gold watches, shining wafers in their palms, 14 carat, thirty-two jewels, fully automatic for just ten-and-six. An old man leaning from the first floor window riffled photographs of fat naked girls, knees obligingly akimbo, showing pubic hair tuftier than shaving brushes, who, though wedged under dark wrestling men, somehow still beamed into the camera.

In Koelietown, van Dam who rolled in pocket-money, bought clothes on the sales. His zoot suits and fancy threads, he called them. Yannovitch searched for a special flick knife he'd once seen in some American movie at the cafe-bioscope, one-and-six a seat plus a green cold drink. I just looked in the windows. Once for ten shillings saved over many months I bought from van Dam a pair of charcoal-grey stove-pipes which he offered to me at a special knock-down price because I was his best friend. The seat was large and shiny and the pants were cut so tightly at the ankles that they looked like jodhpurs but they were mine at least and I hid them from Charity and my mother and smuggled them out to parties under my grey flannels. My mother deeply disapproved of Koelietown which was where, she said, young boys offered their sisters for sale. Of course, that was quite true. And the sisters returned the compliment by putting up their kid brothers wholesale. It was a matter of business, our friend Raboobie of Raboobie's Outfitters in Melkbos Street never tired of assuring us; in Koelietown everything was for sale. There was no such thing as *apartheid*. The only colour that mattered was the colour of a man's money.

"Business, always and only business. It's like a dance, I'm

telling you. The dance of commerce. You've heard of the music of the spheres? The dance of the heavens? Well here we have the dance of the palms." He held up a hand. "These palms. In the dance, the palms press close and speak to each other. And all the palms are pink."

"I never thought of it that way," van Dam said admiringly.

"I am a poet," Raboobie said, "albeit a sadly neglected one."

He was a plump man whose belly piled up behind his white shirtfront like flour and he wore polished winklepickers on his tiny feet though he was in every other way a casual dresser. I never saw him wear anything from his own shop. His hair was careful and gorgeous, thick and glistening, combed back in fat ridges over his ears and he'd so many tiny gold rings with red stones on his fingers that when he ran his hands through his hair, a characteristic gesture as he prepared to press a new suit or shirt on a wavering customer, the red stones winked in the dark hair like brake-lights.

Raboobie worked with a pale, unsmiling boy who did the fetching and carrying. Whenever I saw him he was just leaving. One day he introduced us: "This is my colleague, Shaligram."

Van Dam laughed. "Colleague? But he's a kid."

Raboobie stared. "What do you mean, man? He's fourteen."

"Sounds funny to hear you call him a colleague. He's younger than us." Yannovitch objected. "I'm seventeen. Harry's sixteen."

"I tell you he's my colleague. He does important work. Shaligram is my runner. He runs for me — to collect. He goes to the other shops for alterations and new stock. A good runner is essential. As it is Shaligram is leaving me soon to work for Goolam Brothers who've just opened a big new branch. He wants more money, of course, and a change from counter-work. The Goolams are rich. I can't compete. How will I operate without a runner? That's the trouble with this country, everyone wants to be a boss. Anything else is kaffir work. So if I can't get the stock I need, or the Railways come and say they want to evict me because they need the land then I can go and rot somewhere quietly, you can depend on it. Not so, Shaligram?"

Shaligram smiled for the first time, nodded and slipped out of the door with three pairs of silver-grey slacks over his arm.

"But doesn't he go to school?" I asked.

Raboobie giggled. "Only white people are rich enough to stay at school until they're old men. Shaligram came to me when he was ten. There was a family to help, you see."

Yannovitch was impressed. "Well, if it means getting out of school maybe it's not so bad."

Raboobie leaned confidentially across his counter. "Tell you what. Any time you'd like to give up school, you can come and run for me."

"We couldn't do it," van Dam chipped in hurriedly.

"Why not?" I demanded.

"Well, our mothers wouldn't let us," van Dam said, blushing.

"You're so wet sometimes, I want to puke," Yannovitch told him.

Raboobie laughed and asked him about the knife. It had been going on for years, that business of Yannovitch's search for the flick-knife. It was shaped like a cut-throat razor, he said, with a black bone handle and a little silver button, like a blister, which at the faintest touch sprung a needle point — stiletto. "Tremendously dangerous," van Dam said and Yannovitch said, "Yes, just imagine the accident if it opened in your pocket — it could split a testicle. I'm telling you, just like a toothpick going into a cocktail olive!" And he fell silent for some moments quite overcome by the thought of it. All the time I knew him John was searching for that knife. He was offered others, of course, bowies and super clasps and Japanese flicks in red and green plastic with inlaid golden dragons but they were no good because they opened from the side. He was consistent, old Yannovitch, I'll give him that. He'd accept no substitute. I believe if old Merlin himself had toddled along with an offer of the one true Excalibur, Yannovitch would have asked first if it was shaped like a cut-throat razor and had a bone handle and a little silver button like a blister that made the blade shoot out the front . . .

"Be careful if you ever find that knife," Raboobie warned him. "Flick-knives are illegal. The cops will be after you."

"What else is new? Everything is illegal in this country," Yannovitch said.

"But there's a new man at the Central Police Station. Dekker his name is, a crazy man. He replaces Niewenhuizen, the one who was always after the whores. To him everyone in Koelietown was a whore. This one thinks we're all political. He was in the other day asking about my customers. I told him — I said — you want to know who comes in here? Clerks, washerwomen, students, housewives. And gangsters? he asks. Yes — and gangsters, I say, so what? I sell, they buy. But we don't socialise. I'm a shopkeeper, not a socialite. Don't get cheeky with me you bloody koelie, he says, they may be gangsters today — tomorrow they're terrorists . . .

"One thing leads to another. You just have to spot the connection. If you spot the connection then you come and tell me." Raboobie shook his head. "The only connection I have comes up once a month from Durban in his big car to sell me charcoal trousers. And he's not political either. But you can't tell this Dekker anything. He knows it all."

5

The sunlight striking the bars of my cell makes a hedge of pencil-thin shadows on the paper and into these the clouds drifting across the sun throw round shadows spoked and turning like bicycle wheels so that as I write this I can hear inside my head the creak of the saddle and the scrape of my foot on the tarmac as I walked Mary home in the last week before the final examinations, carrying her bag on my cross-bar while she walked beside me, dainty and sure-footed. I had to stick a leg out to keep my balance, such a snail's progress did we make up the hill to the Ridge and the big gates and gleaming carriage lamps of Mary's house which I had never seen because it lay behind a bend in the long, sandy driveway. I knew that she would have let me kiss her but whenever I screwed up my courage a herd of Great Danes, Dobermans and Alsatians would come thundering around the bend in the drive like runaway coach-horses. Mary told me her father was very concerned about the security of his house. Walking home in the hot afternoons Mary liked to push back her white panama hat with its ribbon in two shades of blue till it hung by its elastic band between her shoulder blades and the tiny bead of sweat I'd first noticed after hockey glinted in the soft down above her lip. When we paused at the stop-streets, I had a brief chance to hold her hand. That's what I was doing on the occasion we met Donally coming from the opposite direction. Donally wore his walking-out black suit and black Homburg. He doffed his hat.

"Who's that?" Mary whispered.

Donally had stopped and was staring after us. He signalled me with a sharp jerk of his head. I left Mary and went over to him. He cocked his head and hissed at me fiercely but carefully as if quite literally determined to keep what he had to say under the brim of his hat.

"Well, would you look at that for a coincidence! Here am I just on my way back from the Seminary, one of heaven's outposts on earth, where the young pupae of the Church hatch into God's brilliant butterflies, his priestly ministers, and who should I meet but a young grub bound for hell. Pull up, Moto! Before it's too late. I warned you, boy, of the fatal pattern you're caught in: first the bad companions, then the lavatory jokes, soon the loose women!" (A flick of the shoulder indicated Mary waiting patiently at the stop-street.) ". . . And then, the drugs . . . sudden death in some lonely room." He sounded a choking little rattle in his throat and rolled his eyes.

"I beg your pardon, Brother — but she's a convent girl."

His voice dropped to a whisper. "Famous last words, Moto. If I were a gambling man I'd not be above laying a pound to a penny that you'll find Martin Luther probably said the same thing about the nun he married. And we know where they finished up." He jerked a thumb at the tarmac. "A very good day to you, Moto."

"Who *is* that?" Mary asked again. "Why is it all brothers look alike?"

"No one," I said.

Mary told me about Goble. "Trevor has strange ideas. He — he says you stole me away from him. I don't like that at all. In the first place it makes it sound as if I belong to him and in the second place it makes you sound like a thief."

"I've been called worse."

"I know. He also says you've got funny blood. And he wants to fight you, that's the rumour. Whatever happens I want you to promise me you won't fight him."

"I promise."

It was easy enough to say. I wondered what would happen if Goble was prepared to overlook my promise and began hitting me.

In the last week before the examination Donally was before us in all his wonderful faces, looking forward to our eternal ruin and perdition. He took to referring to it as the Last

Judgment or, quite simply, the Drop. The idea of the matriculation dance following on the Saturday night clearly displeased him. He called it a useless pleasure, the last cigarette for a condemned man. It took him the entire last period to say goodbye to us and he obviously enjoyed it; it made him feel, he said, rather like the angel who will harry the sinners to the Judgment Seat on the last day, and then he rounded off with a second recital of The Angelus which he had Greenbaum recite although the time was by then almost three. Just for luck, he said, and at the end he appealed on our behalf to St Jude, patron saint of hopeless cases, in a long prayer from the scaffold. The class schloeps cheered him mightily when he washed his hands of us and Mother's Little went scooting off and returned with his lunch box slopping water so Donally could actually do it properly, which of course he did with gusto, splashing about like a kid at the seaside and drying his hands on his cassock.

Judgment Day was nine sharp on Monday morning. But mine came rather sooner. Instead of St Michael, or Gabriel, or whoever is supposed to urge along the resurrected to the Judgment Seat, making sure that no one is hiding in the toilets, there was Goble, all six thick feet of him, leaning up against the wire fence around the bike shed, his socks down showing fat, unhealthy, pallid, hairless calves, thumbs hooked into his belt. He was gnawing his bottom lip. A habit of Goble's, that gnawing. Even under his big black drum-major's busby covering half his face, marching ahead of the school bugle band twirling his mace topped with the silver thistle, you knew it could only be Goble simply by those teeth working at the lip. He kind of fed on himself and all that fat went straight on his calves.

Yannovitch coming up behind barged into me.

"What you waiting for, Harry?" Then he whispered right in my ear-hole, "Keerist!" And I knew he'd seen Goble. "I warned you, Harry, didn't I? I fuckin' warned you, my mate."

Slowly, as if he hated having to do it, Goble let go of his lower lip. "I hear you been making a play for my chick, Moto. That was stupid. You lost your marbles."

"And who says?"

"I say. Mary's got better things to do than hanging around

with a little coffee-coloured creep who gives the impression his old lady was jumped by a garden boy. With your complexion, crissy hair and all, next to you even my kaffir girl's good looking." And he went back to eating his lip.

Yannovitch was jumping up and down at my elbow. "Jesus, Harry, you can't let him say that about your Mom!"

"You keep out of this you mad Slav," Goble said, "or I might do you as well."

"Oh yes?" Yannovitch pushed me out of the way and shoved his nose dangerously close to Goble's sharp little teeth. "You and whose army?"

"Listen," Goble shouted, "I could take on the pair of you with one hand tied behind my back!"

"Right," said Yannovitch.

We went down to the rugby field with a whole crowd trooping behind us. They made a circle.

Goble faced us, his feet planted like tree trunks. I could see the muscles bulging in his calves. His arms were stretched rigid by his side ending in fists the size of feet. He was grinding his teeth like an epileptic. "Anything goes?" he asked.

"Well, not *anything*," I said, "no kicking."

"Anything goes," Yannovitch nodded.

Goble put his head down, molars gnashing, and roaring in his nose he came at us like a tank. Me, I just watched. There didn't seem anything else to do. When he hits me, I remember thinking, I'll pretend to be dead — if I'm not dead already.

He never got near me. Yannovitch waited until he was almost on us and then he dropped, caught Goble around the knees and brought him down like a brick wall, face first.

"Quick Harry, pin him!"

I collapsed on Goble's back. Maybe the fall had stunned him or something because he didn't move. He just lay there, kicking a bit and mooing like a cow waiting for the branding iron, the whites showing big in his eyes, dust covering the underside of his face and powdering his torn lip, mixing with the blood in the corner. Yannovitch pushed me off and took over, twisting Goble's arms behind him. I heard them crack in their sockets. Goble thrashed about in a feeble sort of way.

I crawled around and peered into one staring eye. Then I hit him pretty hard in the corner of his mouth where the blood was. Next I hit him in the eye. It closed. I began to feel sick. The crowd who had been shouting a bit when the fight started kept quiet now.

"The other side, Harry. Knock the shit out of him."

I took a handful of hair and screwed Goble's face around. Half of me still couldn't believe it really was big Goble just lying there letting little me hit him. I felt sure it was just a question of time before he jumped up and strangled the two of us. A part of me wanted to start throwing up. Instead, I took aim at his mouth where the dust caked in the lips and hit him again while his one good eye watched.

"That's for what he said about your Mom," Yannovitch told me.

When I thought about it afterwards I decided that it wasn't for her so much that I did it. My old lady could take care of herself. What really made me mad was Goble's crack about the garden boy. There must have been more of my father in me than I've cared to admit. The thing that rankled was that we had never had a garden boy.

Shuckel's behaviour during the maths paper disturbed me badly. After spending ages staring out of the window, suddenly he'd make lightning calculations on his rough paper, and with a fat slap of his ruler draw heavy lines under the answer which I knew would be correct to about nine decimal places, all the time smirking horribly and turning to me with snapturtle winks and giving the thumbs-up until, thank God, the invigilator saw him and made him stop.

Fatty Wyner finished his Latin paper a full hour before anybody else.

Van Dam spent a lot of time staring at the ceiling. Obviously he knew nothing.

I pinned everything on the English exam. There I had a head start because I actually liked reading. Most guys never stretched to more than *Superman* comics and *Prince Valiant*. Even Shuckel, who was some kind of intellectual, read only politics. Yannovitch always read aloud, Jack Wyner moved his lips and van Dam would point his finger.

I had taken trouble to get up an essay beforehand. These were pretty easy to "spot". Usual sort of titles: " 'Twas the Night Before Christmas", "My Holiday In Durban", "On

Safari", "In The Farmyard", "First Snow", "Oh To Be In England" . . . I plumped for the old farm. Of course you can't have a farm without a drought. There were always prayer services for rain going on in some part of the country where once again the drought was the worst in living memory, sheep coughing their last, dongas deepening, dust rising, last showers in the year of the Great Trek. It was a good theme. Always topical. Each Christmas you'd see the new books in the CNA windows: *The Drought of Love*, *Too Late The Deluge*, *The Thirsty Years* . . .

When the time came I was ready with my memorised lead-in:

> . . . *The sun blazed from a gun-blue sky. Oom Koos sat on his stoep staring out across his farm with rheumy eyes. A dung-beetle rolled its big ball across the baking ground, getting his shoulder behind it like a good lock-forward. There was little left for that dung-beetle, Oom Koos reflected. And there was nothing left for him. Six sheep lost in as many days. One he found in the dust at the bottom of the donga. The jackals had been busy. The Lord gave and the Lord took away. He'd taken his best ewes that he'd saved four years to buy. He'd taken Tante Mina, too. But He had given no rain in return. Perhaps Mina's passing had been a kindness. He had to break the veld to make her grave. He couldn't cry when he put her in the earth. To let tears drop on the dying veld seemed a crime. For ten long years the heavens had burnt. The Long Thirst, the Bantu called it. He prayed that God would take him soon — that he wouldn't be there to see the vultures at the eyes of his sheep . . .*

When I got the paper I found that the essay title was "Happy Days On The Farm". No sweat. There is this boy, see, who is incredibly happy on this farm until he has this incredibly unhappy dream about Oom Koos . . .

6

Looking back to the big night of the matric dance I tremble at my ignorance, my gullibility. If one considers ignorance and gullibility as broad streams, then I was their confluence. There is an official stamp on my ignorance: I never did discover if I passed the matriculation examination. As to gullibility — well neither did I ever get my money back on the useless hair-straightening lotion. If any further evidence is needed of the lame-brain I was it is to be found in the fact that it never occurred to me that the dance was not something separate from the exams we'd just finished: it was one of them and it was one of the tests I failed hopelessly. But I was desperately in love. More than ever before in my life I wanted things to go right. At the time in my callow way, as I saw things, I had problems to solve if I was to go to the dance and put a decent face on it. In fact, as I soon discovered, my real problem was simply surviving at all. As things are now I'm not sure if I'm going to make it.

I bought from the chemist something called African Dream. Two tubes of pungent cream in a box gaudy with the Stars and Stripes and loud with promises.

Men — Women! For The Straightest Hair You've Ever Seen! Tonite Will Be Your African Dream! ONE SHOT ONE STOP OVERNIGHT TREATMENT — OR YOUR MONEY BACK!!

Late on Friday night before the dance I slopped a bucket of warm water into my room, locked the door and gave my scrubby mop the full treatment.

Putting it bluntly, at that time I was about as thick as two planks, solid bone from forehead to the back wall of the court. I spent weeks working on the problem of my flat-iron feet. The old trotters, together with the fact that I couldn't dance a step, should have been enough to keep me rooted to the spot all evening. Would that they had done so! But, madman that I was, I'd worked on my deficiencies, doubling my arch exercises and trying something new, stepping out after dark and walking around the block a couple of times each evening on tip-toes. I borrowed a book from the library and stumbled after the black and white dance steps weaving across the page like animal spoor around a busy waterhole, clutching my pillow to my chest, counting time to the radio which, between rugby commentaries, police reports and political broadcasts played nothing but Mantovani and Victor Sylvester and more Mantovani. Realising that I hadn't a hope of getting the hang of things, but telling myself I'd muddle through somehow if only I had the feeling of the business in hand, I battled on. I did my breathing exercises religiously and tried to stop looking at my bust sideways in the mirror.

There was the question of transport. How was I to get Mary to the dance? I thought for about half a second of asking my father to "take" us in his old green Consul, fondly called "the bus". He and my mother took Sunday afternoon drives in it, nursing the old engine along, hissing like a kettle, twenty miles top limit, out along the national road near Rustenburg and then back home again squinting into the five o'clock sun with my old man rolling down the window to curse the drivers who passed him, waving his fist. I can hear him now — "Flash Harry!" and "Bloody cowboys!" There was no guarantee that he wouldn't behave as badly on the drive to the school hall. In the end I drew out all the money in my post office account and ordered a taxi.

There was the problem of what to wear. My mother dug out my father's old dress suit which he had not worn, as I discovered from the ticket in the pocket, since an El Alamein reunion at the MOTH hall in Berea in 1952.

"Why throw money away on a new suit?" my mother wanted to know, always the soul of patience in these matters. "It will only hang in your cupboard for years on end waiting for the moth and the mould — after all, it's not as if you go to special dances every night of the week."

I held the suit against me. The trousers were miles too long and the waist was big enough for three of me.

"Please note the wide lapels." My father pointed them out to my mother, turning me this way and that to catch the light better, as if he were handling an empty suit. "The fashion's coming back, I believe."

"Would it be too much to ask you to thank your father for his kind offer?" my mother demanded gently. "I'll take up the trousers for you and the cummerband will hide any looseness around your middle — though I must say," she said as she inspected me closely, "you're too thin, Harry. My guess is you don't eat properly. You prefer indulging in white bread, Coca-Cola and fish and chips — like the natives do . . . no wonder you're short for your age."

My father was staring at the suit and his eyes were misty. "It's Savile Row, of course. Seen some good times, that outfit, some good shows — before the war."

"For heaven's sake! Why put ideas into the child's head?" my mother demanded through a mouthful of pins. "Harry hasn't seen fit to tell us who he's taking to this so-called dance, but you'll be the first to complain if there is any monkey business."

I completed the African Dream treatment, wrapped a towel around it, practised the fox-trot for an hour and then took a look in the mirror. Where before I wore in place of a decent head of hair a tightly woven mop of rusty wire bunched like a fist, now the mop had collapsed and in its place a cap of large, sleek coils hung about my ears. I towelled it vigorously but it didn't help though the dye badly stained the towel. I pushed it into the back of a drawer. In a state of horror I went to bed and slept badly.

It was no better in the morning. Fluffy, black, broken-backed wedges stuck out around my head like a child's toy windmill. Wearing the best face I could muster beneath it I went to breakfast, Harry the human gollywog, whistling between dry lips.

My father was already in his place sawing through his bacon. My mother hovered in attendance. She always got breakfast on Saturday, it being Charity's lying-in morning.

"How many times have I told you not to whistle at the table?" my father demanded without looking up, busily amputating his bacon rind.

My mother stared. Then she closed her eyes. "Harry! For

68

pity's sake — what have you done? You look like . . ." she opened her eyes, "like an Indian shopkeeper."

My father looked up. He passed a hand in front of his face. "God, oh God!" he said with a mouth full of bacon and egg.

"I suppose this is one of your modern tricks?" My mother's voice was icy. "Harry, I'm ashamed of you."

"Do you mean this?" I patted the slack, oily curls.

"God in heaven!" My old man threw down his knife and fork. "What else?" He jumped up from the table and rushed out into the garden.

"It's *my* hair," I called after him. "I'm the one who has to live with it."

In the silence that followed I could hear him turn on the hose. When he got mad he watered the garden or dug up weeds. Funny thing is — the garden survived on my father's rages.

"It's not the colour I hate. More the texture. It's like wire. And what with my dark skin, well, it makes me feel not quite . . . *right*, if you know what I mean. Here, feel it yourself." I held out a fistful to my mother.

"Jesus!" my old man shrieked from the passage where he'd been hiding and listening after sneaking in from the garden to give me a stir in case I'd cooled down. "What bloody bare-faced cheek! He comes in here looking like an Abo from the bush, then he blames us for it!" He rushed out again.

My mother began to cry. "How can you say things like this to your own mother and father? And you who were such a lovely boy as a baby."

Through the window I watched my old man rushing at the roses with the aphid spray, pumping furiously, soon surrounded by a cloud of pesticide so thick he moved inside it like a ghost.

There was no talking to my mother in tears. She hid behind them. I moved the cold food around my plate.

I spent the morning sitting on the front verandah, my feet up on the wall, doing my chest exercises. I didn't imagine they'd help me but they calmed my nerves. The fresh air made me feel light-headed, and gladly befuddled I gulped it in by the lungful and exhaled noisy steam-engine puffs into the bright, empty morning while my father moved furiously about the garden with great destructive energy. He carried a bucket and an old screwdriver and every so often he got down on one knee and attacked the weeds carpeting the yellow, scurvy grass. Wresting a weed from the ground he'd smash it with a clang on the rim of the bucket, spattering the hard little clods of earth the roots had drawn up. The weeds, rank, green and powerful, were of a much higher order than the grass they choked; a sparse and scaly fuzz, its little roots got the merest toe-hold in the acidic shale. Pulling the weeds did great damage to the little baking patch of jaundiced stubble we called the front lawn. I watched my father moving across this desert like an air-raid, leaving scrabbled craters where the weeds had been, into which the sunlight poured like hot, white water.

In front of me a couple of steps led down to the garden-path. It was at the foot of the steps that Charity presented herself around mid-morning carrying the stained towel I'd used the night before. She stood and stared at me. My father, seeing her and sensing something was up, hurried off to fetch my mother, coughing loudly and spitting phlegm among the flowers. The towel was dripping wet and it took me a few moments to realise that she had been washing it. My father came back with my mother who was still crying. She had been crying since breakfast as if it had become something semi-permanent like a cold, that she couldn't shake off. Grey-faced, Charity held up the towel and wrung it out and water hit the hot slate path. Then she gave it a shake and there were the stains, still very black. No one said anything. There was no need to. They looked at me and my funny hair and I looked at the stains. I knew the way it was. Admit for half a moment that you're anything less than snow-white and someone shoves a leper bell in your hand and the world rushes off in the opposite direction shrieking "Unclean! Unclean!" Of course, deep down in their heart of hearts, half the country believes the other half does in fact suffer from a touch of the tarbrush. But it's something you keep to yourself — unless you're looking for a fight. No, there wasn't any need for words. By my desperate attempt to straighten my hair I had brought into the open a dreadful secret my parents must have known about and tried to hide. They stared at me as if the skeleton in the closet had put on flesh and was swinging from the lower branches of the family tree. Charity was staring at all of us as if she had suddenly discovered she was working for a family of Coloureds — which in her book would have been even lower than working for Indians. I stared at my feet and continued my exercises.

Charity wrung out the towel again for good measure. Then my mother and father moved off down the garden path, slow and grave, like a couple of gun-carriages in a state funeral, she weeping and he spitting into the flowers, and somehow I kept breathing.

I decided to brazen out lunch. This turned out to be a bad mistake. We ate roast lamb, see, and my father came in from the garden, forgot to take his hat off and stood there hacking bits of the dead lamb with a blunt carving knife while my mother screwed her hankie into the corner of her mouth to stifle her sobs. Then two flies began copulating noisily around the lights above the table. But nobody, dammit, said a word. Mind you, what with the flies buzzing excitedly and pinging into the lightbulb, my mother's sniffs and the old man breathing through his nose it was a noisy enough lunch and so hot I had the feeling we were eating in the oven from which the lamb had come. As we were finishing Charity arrived carrying exhibit A, turning it this way and that like an auctioneer so we should get the full horror of it. My father and mother nodded sadly and Charity reversed out of the room. Let me tell you that never, since Veronica went to work on the road to Calvary, has anyone snaffled so much mileage out of a towel.

My father's suit hung behind the door smelling of must and the meths my mother had used to clean it. It had begun to fossilise after years of disuse and crackled softly as I eased my way inside. I tightened the cummerband with a cunning arrangement of knots and pins and took up most of the slack in the trouser waist but the seat swung baggily in parachute folds. I estimated that, luckily enough, the length of the jacket would help to cover most of the slack. My hair had settled more heavily on my head and looked dismayingly like a rather cheap wig. My mother and father had locked themselves in the living room and were listening to the radio. Vera Lynne was singing "The White Cliffs of Dover". It almost muffled the sound of my mother's sobs. I took a last look at my book of dance steps, snapped on my fake bow-tie and stepped into the night.

The taxi was not the low-slung, black job I'd fondly imagined. I waited at the front gate and a battered blue Zephyr aiming an enormous pink butterfly cruised up to me. The driver was a pale little guy with the sort of skin you get on hot milk. He consulted a scrap of paper. "Name of Moto? Cab for the College. Party to collect on the Ridge? Hop in chief, before the cops lumber you for loitering." The back seat was covered with leopard skin and lumpy with springs. I leaned back, closed my eyes, fiddled with my tie, feeling my bowels loosening.

I wanted to turn back immediately we arrived. Carriage lamps gleamed on the white stone gate-posts, on the brass buttons of the khaki uniform of the nightwatchman saluting with his knobkerrie as the Zephyr, pink butterfly straining at the moon, swept up what seemed like a mile of paved drive-way. On my right was the high webbing of a tennis court, to my left the dark slick of a swimming pool and behind every bush and shrub the soft yellow glow of concealed lighting. Even the driver was impressed. "Hoity toity!" he muttered over his shoulder.

"Please wait. I may be a while. On no account hoot."

"Suits me, squire. Waiting goes on the meter, see."

Mary let me in. Her blue dress seemed to make her shimmer from the shoulders down. But then, perhaps I was shaking. Either way, the air between us was on the move and I saw her white shoulders and neck rippling above the blue. Her hair was dressed in a high, complicated style. I don't remember clearly many details of our meeting. But even now her shoes come back to me — blue satin with tiny heels showing a soft, furred gleam in the sharp electric light of the hallway. Her dress clung to her small, high breasts and was held there by a single strap looping in a figure eight around her neck.

She examined me minutely with her head on one side. "You've done something to your hair."

"It wouldn't lie down. I decided to take it in hand. I'm afraid things didn't go quite according to plan."

She nodded. "Still, it looks like you won. It's an interesting effect. Dark, in a slightly sinister sort of way and rather — loose." She considered a moment, finger on chin. "Shadowy.

That's it. Rather shadowy, you are. As if when someone shone a bright light you'd disappear. Fade out." She reached out a hand quickly as if to reassure herself it wouldn't happen and patted my lapel. "I've never been out with anyone in a dress suit."

"It's Savile Row. My father's actually. He lent it to me."

"That was kind of him."

"He absolutely insisted. He's a tall chap."

"So I see." Her eyes measured the suit, subtracted me and dwelt on the remainder. "Poor Harry. You look so thin — and mysterious. I've always thought of you as brown and wiry. It's as if you were in disguise." She eyed the black concertinas resting on my shoes. "What have you done to take up the slack?"

I patted my middle. "Tucked behind the cummerband and pinned. Afraid I could be some trouble on the dance floor." I tried for a nonchalant laugh and there issued from my parched lips the rusty whisper of a waterless tap. "What I mean is, I'm not quite cut out for the old Hokey Pokey. I may not even make the most gentle waltz. Sorry . . . but one false move could be disastrous. These pants wouldn't touch my knees on the way down."

She looked delighted. "Hang on to me. I'm a strong dancer."

"Oh, I will, I will."

"Come and meet Daddy. He's in a very bad mood. He's just had a new burglar alarm installed and it doesn't work. He's enormously worried about security. We're forever being robbed, you see. We have dogs, watchmen, guns — none of it seems to make the slightest difference. We still get burglars the way other people have mice. By the way, do you want Daddy to drive us to the dance?"

"Thank you," I said in my iciest voice, "but I have a car."

"Good. Daddy will be relieved. He can keep working on the alarm. Come and meet him while I do a bit of fiddling with my hair." She turned with a rustle of stiff petticoats and led me into the living room.

Her father was at the picture window, which was criss-crossed with glinting strands of wire. A plump guy in khaki shorts with peppercorn hair, he sat twanging the wire and listening anxiously. "Young Moto, is it?" he asked without turning around. "Sit yourself down."

I sat in a salmon-pink armchair, well *sank*, really, up to my armpits, elbows level with my ears. Panelled in dark wood and plushly carpeted, it was a hushed and solid room. Wyner's house had carpets just like it. You left prints, which Wyner always said looked like snow tracks. He should have known because once when he'd been driving with his folks down to Queenstown for a cousin's wedding, snow had fallen, unaccountably, on the side of the national road. He'd got out and actually rooted around in the stuff. Imagine that! It made him the only guy who'd ever seen snow. For that alone he'd joined the ranks of the famous ones — Bobo Vermeulen who'd been to America and old Ralphie Blenkinsop whose big brother worked for the television service in England. Wyner was famous for his account of the snow. People use to come up to him shyly at school and ask in tones of huge wonder if what they had heard was true and Jack never tired of telling the story. Sitting in the hot, dusty playground, pausing only to wipe the sweat out of his eyebrows, he would tell his huge-eyed listeners of the time the magic white stuff had unaccountably fallen on the side of the national road to Queenstown. I sat staring at my snowtracks in the deep pile that led to the soft, salmon-pink armchair, hoping Mary would be quick, praying the taxi-driver would not lose patience or start hooting, and listening to Mr Smithson strumming and twanging an unhappy little tune on the burglar alarm wire. He appeared to have forgotten about me.

"This is a nice place you've got here, Mr Smithson."

"It should be," he said promptly. "I've worked damn hard for it. There's twenty years of solid sweat tied up in what you see around you." He turned around and took me in for the first time. "Good God — you're in a monkey suit! Jolly good show, getting decently togged for this do tonight. Somebody's got to keep up standards. The old formalities are going one by one. Soon we shall be sitting around in our birthday suits eating porridge — just like our black brethren. And that's when they'll strike. I mean you can't fight back with a dish of *putu* in your lap, not so? By the way, I think I knew your family — or a part of it."

"Surely not. As a family we're pretty well unknown. I

mean, speaking as one of them, I can say we've never been heard of."

"No, I knew your Dad of old. Mind you, you're much darker than he is. We were at Sidi Rezegh together. How's the old insurance game? He sold me a packet a few years back. I said to him at the time, I said — we live and learn. What a price to put on my head! When we were up North I wouldn't have given you twopence for it. A sound chap, your Dad. Knight of the Road. Of course, my life is worth many thousands of twopences now. Ah . . . I've come a long way from the days when I didn't have two of 'em to rub together. Ever kept goldfish, young Moto? They cost about twopence apiece, y'know, before the war. I kept an aquarium by the window over there. Poor little buggers had to go to make way for the wire when I put in this alarm. See that white patch on the wall? That's where I had 'em. Wife said they stank. But I loved them, bright flashy things, twopence a piece. My wife, that's Mrs Smithson, she's upstairs with a migraine. I think the failure of this damn alarm brought it on. We agonised for hours over which system to choose — Tarson or Pluto, Reveille or Mantrap, which was it to be? Wire or metal strips? Bell or siren? Oh, the argument raged this way and that. We must have protection, you understand? Especially since the shooting. We've got a dog, of course, Rufus, German Wolfhound, kennelled in the servants' yard by night. I mean, *when* they come, that's the way they'll come, isn't it? Then there's the nightwatchman, Phineas, at the gate, for what he's worth. You'll have seen him when you arrived. I've set spotlights on the roof, north and south. In my cupboard, in the sock drawer actually, don't tell a soul, I've my old service revolver, army issue Browning, pulls to the left, but good enough for the purpose and we've had burglar bars up for ages, naturally. But *still* the bastards break in. Found this Johnny at my window not two nights ago working the old fishing rod trick, line and hook through the window, going for my trousers. Damn near lifted 'em clear when he had the bad luck to snare the blanket. Freezing backside woke me up. I yelled. Wife yelled. Dived into the sock drawer and chased him. He went over the wall like a springbok, all ten foot of it. Once outside he must have thought he'd shaken me but I went through the side gate. He paused by the roadside. Fatal. I potted him and dragged him into the garden. Always remember that — if you shoot a coon be sure it's on your own land. At that moment old Phineas the watchman comes ambling up. Typical. Never there when you want them. 'What shall I do with this rubbish, baas?' he says, turning him over with his foot. Merciless to their own kind, y'know. Well . . . problem. What *do* you do with a dead kaffir at three in the morning? The police weren't interested. He'll keep till morning, they said. So I had to leave him on the lawn. A helluva thing, that. Us tucked up between the sheets and him stiff among the dahlias. Still, that's life, I suppose. Well, after that there was no question about it, we had to have a decent alarm. So the chappies came in and wired the place, worked like beavers to finish by last night, connected it up to a great clanging bell, packed up and left, it being the weekend. I come along to test it just now, jiggle the wire and blow-all happens." He waved his pliers hopelessly and then turned to me with sad eyes. "I've tinkered, but . . . it's an integrated system. Absolutely the latest thing. In theory the slightest touch sets it off; brushing up against a drainpipe, tapping a window, say — the house lights blaze, bell hammers away and the old panic button's well and truly hit down at the local cop-shop to which we're linked by private land line and in two minutes flat the boys in blue are backing the Black Maria up to the door." He sighed. "By the same token, it looks as if when one thing blows the whole system goes up the spout. One faulty connection and it means checking the whole shebang."

Mary shimmered into the room and kissed him on his grizzled curls. I eased myself out of the armchair, adjusted my cummerband and we said goodbye.

"No loose Africans wandering about the place — are there Moto?" He gestured towards the night beyond the picture window with an anxious bob of his head.

Mary raised her eyes to the ceiling. "For heaven's sake Daddy — why on earth should there be Africans about at the school dance?"

"Because they're everywhere, that's why. Just look at those girls forever being pounced on in parked cars down by Lovers' Lake. And let me tell you, it's no good crying after you've been criminally assaulted. It's too late then. You'll agree with me, Moto. Prevention — that's the thing. Being the son of an insurance man, your father will have told you — you don't get cover against rape."

"I'll keep my eyes open, sir."

But he had stopped listening and was back at work on the delicate wires that veined the windows, his pliers' head a wicked little snake, darting and nipping, searching out the faulty connection.

In the taxi such was the lumpiness of the ill-sprung, yellow leopard-skin seats that we fell against each other as the car took off and stayed like that, awkwardly propped and pleasantly close, on adjacent camel humps. When Mary's hair, that looked so soft and gleaming, brushed my cheek, it felt surprisingly hard and sticky with the consistency of meringue. But then it was to be an evening of shocks.

"Daddy has an obsession about security and natives. He believes they're everywhere just waiting to do him in."

"They *are* everywhere," the driver interjected.

I tapped him on the shoulder. "Drive."

"Charming," he muttered.

It was as we passed Phineas at the gate knocking at his cap-peak with his knobkerrie in sleepy salute that the night was suddenly torn in two by a great, clanging bell. Minutes later a police-van hurtled past us. Evidently Mr Smithsom had made the connection.

"The police won't be too pleased with your father."

"He won't care. As far as he's concerned it's simply their job to come when he calls. He thinks of daily life as a war and of the police as his private army." I felt her tense against me. "It will make Mummy's migraine worse, though. You know, sometimes I feel completely alone in a world full of madmen. Everything is a question of black and white. There is nothing else." She turned to me with a little helpless laugh. "Honestly, you'd think we were still fighting the Kaffir Wars . . ."

The driver didn't say anything to that but he could not resist nodding heavily in agreement. I felt her shiver and put an arm around her, not simply because I liked her, which I did, but because I was suddenly sorry for her, and I kept my arm around her all the way to the college despite the fact that it seriously disturbed our complex balance on the camel humps. The driver was clearly watching every move in his mirror.

There were few public events we Bonaventurians took part in and even fewer we enjoyed. We enjoyed least the thrashings in front of the school — but I do not speak for such ghouls as P. Litnavatov, the white Russian from Rustenburg. Litnavatov was nearly expelled for paying junior boys to tie him stark naked to the parallel bars in the gym and beat him with the backs of cricket gloves — behaviour inspired, he insisted, by the fiery sermons on the mortification of the flesh (with slides) given in religious instruction by Brother Phelan, better known as the mad monk from Cork. Rather more happy were the frequent rugby matches against local Afrikaans school teams, holy wars, in fact, giving both sides, players and spectators, a chance to work off steam and smite a blow for their God. Encounters we customarily lost: mainly, I suspect, because our people were queasy about tackling chaps who invariably looked old enough to be their fathers, displaying here and there a fully formed moustache, receding hairlines and many skins a richer, darker tone even than mine. The occasional death of one of the Brothers was always immensely popular for the half-day mourning it immediately earned. But top of the league were the matriculation dances, unrivalled for glamour, excitement and fierce competition, with each year's leavers trying to transform the great brick and iron aeroplane hangar of the school hall with flags, flowers, bunting and papier mâché into a fairground, a Swiss Alp, a rodeo, or a desert island, spurred on by the ambition to make the efforts of the previous year's matriculants look like a nuns' Tupperware party. In the face of the fever this aroused in the school and the folk memories it triggered in the Brothers of medieval villages driven completely beserk, celebrating amid virgins and poteen the feast days of doubtful saints, stringent rules decreed that no one should smoke or drink or go outside during the dance, with the inevitable result that quite naturally everyone worth his salt was expected to do all three, and preferably simultaneously.

In our year they changed the rules. The news came to us in the persons of Goble, Smees and Gebhardt.

"We're a deputation from your committee," Gebhardt announced.

"Hello, Trev." I tried to sound bright and positive.

"You whimpering prick," he said.

"Your committee has made a deal with the Brothers for the night of the dance. We behave and they'll stay home. No smoking, drinking, or groping in the bushes and we'll not see a dog-collar all night." Smees beamed proudly.

"One day someone's going to kill you, Goble," Yannovitch said.

"Now we didn't come to fight," said Gebhardt, backing away. "We came to warn you, that's all. So now you know."

"You can't say we didn't warn you," Smees offered from a distance. "And we'll be watching."

Goble didn't say anything until the deputation was a long way off and then he turned and bawled, "We'll be watching you; bloody sure we will!"

A sad departure from the heady yesteryears then, our matric dance, planned not by the class as a whole but by a committee of schloeps who took over in a bloodless coup by the simple, effective expedient of printing the tickets well in advance and refusing to sell them to the bad eggs unless those so designated agreed to leave all arrangements to said committee. The brains behind the move was Kenny Darling. This possibly explained — together with his altar-service link — why Jack Wyner was allowed onto the committee as a menial, working long hours polishing floors and laying tables, though he was booted out the night before it all happened, when the big props arrived, so he wouldn't be able to blab: all he could tell us was that the theme was to be FLYING HIGH and he'd had to blow up a lot of balloons and swore that as a result he'd broken a lot of small veins in his neck.

Kenny Darling announced his intention of coming to the dance despite the fact that he had entered the seminary immediately after the exams and had to get special permission from the Archbishop. We went along to see him installed at the urging of Yannovitch who said that, after all, in a country so starved of high jinks that people would queue to watch aeroplanes taking off, the chance of seeing a man putting by the world, the flesh and devil was not to be sniffed at; and van Dam whose word usually carried in religious matters because he had a second cousin who was a nun, predicted an impressive ceremony; it would be rather like seeing the Russians and Americans on Movietone News exchanging spies at Checkpoint Charlie in Berlin.

We toiled up the steep hill to the top of the Ridge and the choice site occupied by the Seminary of St Peter the Martyr thrusting out of the soft green hillside above the city in a series of interlocking block houses dominated by the chapel with its giant Norman tower in concrete, studded with large pebbles and surrounded by a red brick wall topped with broken glass. God's fortress and barracks was St Peter's, built in the days when the war against the Romans was hotting up and the far-sighted fathers knew they'd better build tall and strong against the day that the Calvinists began the pogrom and it would be well to command the high ground. As it turned out, the handing over of Mother's Little wasn't the event we anticipated. He arrived in his mother's biscuit Chevrolet with the imitation shrunken head dangling from the driving mirror. We leaned on our bicycles in the shade of a jacaranda tree. Spotting us, Little Darlin' turned his face to the afternoon sun for added radiance and stood dumbly by while his mother unpacked from the boot all his worldly possessions and loaded him to the heavens with paper bags, prayer books, cake tins, a large statue of the Virgin and piles of underwear, turned the lad smartly around and wheeled him up the cement path like she was handling a stuffed supermarket trolley. And the big, mailed doors banged behind him.

We caused quite a stir when we stepped from the taxi outside the school hall. There was some sardonic applause from the crowd and whistles for my hair. I paid the cabbie and asked him to collect us at midnight. "Sure thing, my old chief," and he gave a horrible smirk, "don't do anything I wouldn't." I was sweating in the suit and the trousers stuck to my thighs and pulled uncomfortably on the pins and tucks. Goble was at the door. I gave him our ticket. "Good evening, Trevor," Mary said in a clear voice, and then more loudly still: "Is that enough? Or would you like to see Harry's Identity Card as well?" Then I knew she'd heard about the fight. Goble said nothing but he blushed a little and licked nervously at the tooth marks in his upper lip.

Van Dam had come with Dottie who wore this Roman matron's costume of petal pink, her smiling creases smothered in face-powder. Shuckel, red hair winking like a traffic light, was beside Mina, dressed entirely in yellow, hair drawn up over her head and shaped like a club. She gave me a tight little smile like a grinning lemon. Yannovitch, busily lacing a glass of Coke from a large silver hipflask, was dressed to kill in a white sportscoat with padded shoulders, hanging to his knees, and charcoal stovepipes taken in so tightly they showed the bulge of his calves. He laughed so much when he saw me that his Bill Haley kisscurls shook over his brow. When he turned I noticed the grey streaks sprayed into his sideboards. He introduced his girl with a pat on the bottom. "Meet Rochelle. That there's Mary Smithson and the penguin next to her is Harry Moto. Excuse his hair. I think he must be wearing a wig."

Rochelle giggled. She pointed a long silver fingernail at my middle. "My Dad's got one of those suits. He wears it when he goes to the Masons."

"What's his name? Perhaps I've bumped into him at Lodge meetings."

For a moment I thought I had her. Her lips actually formed the name, then she shook her head. "Oh crap, man! You're having me on." And she laughed, big white teeth appearing suddenly between her lips like rabbits at the door of their hutch.

Nobody else was amused. If anything more was needed to set Rochelle aside — that was it. In the good Catholic community, such as we were, Mason, like Calvinist or abortionist was one of the words that made girls cross their legs and tough boys blush and mutter into their shirt fronts.

Only Jack Wyner offered some contrast to Yannovitch, since van Dam and Shuckel had come in what I guessed by the turned-down turn-ups of their dark grey trousers would be their old confirmation suits. Even so, Wyner looked totally ridiculous in a wine red tuxedo and blue spotted bow-tie. No doubt, along with the baseball bat, another present from his uncle in America. He introduced this girl, Sheila. "She has the weekend off — from Kingsmead." Now none of us had ever heard of the place but we knew from the tone that it was *Up*. From what ever world Sheila had stepped her look told you that this one definitely gave her trouble breathing.

As we moved off in search of a table van Dam dropped a word in my ear. "If I were you Moto, I'd sit down quickly and not show myself again. In that outfit you'll have people ordering drinks off you."

"So pleased you could accompany the Queen Mother tonight," I whispered, "she so gracious and serene and you traipsing along behind her in that boring suit like her private detective."

"But seriously, what have you done to your hair? It's nasty, man."

"Look, can we shut up about my hair? I mean, how would you like it if you had hair like mine? I tried to straighten it out — and it didn't work."

"It looks like a hat. No, wait a minute — I lie — it looks like you're wearing a tea-cosy. Except I've never seen a black tea-cosy."

To be honest the old school hall wasn't half bad. Certainly it had been transformed from the pit of a place we'd sweated in through the exams for a long hot fortnight. The floor, buffed to a gleam, glittered and shimmered, reflecting swollen bunches of balloons swinging from the roof. Everywhere smelt of polish, perfume and hair-oil. The big spectacular decoration against sight of which Wyner had been booted out the night before soared overhead throwing a giant trembling shadow as far as the stage; it was nothing less than a full-size model of a fighter plane painted in black and silver. A Spitfire someone said. Upon the flower-banked stage Hennie Koekemoer And His Trio swung through "Cherry Pink And Appleblossom White" in sheepskin flying jackets with Hennie himself out front in a leather flying helmet, all dangling ear-flaps, lifting his trumpet like a strangely shrunken, emaciated elephant blaring through his skimpy metal trunk. Behind the Koekemoer Trio was a message in letters several feet high sprayed on the blue velvet stage curtains in fake Christmas snow:

ST BONAVENTURE MATRICULATION 1959
TAKING OFF! FLYING HIGH! GOD BLESS!

"Who damaged the curtains?" Shuckel demanded and we could tell from his injured tone that he was as impressed as the rest of us.

"You're jealous," Mina said flatly.

Mother's Little sat at the head of a table of cronies, splendid in his new, black, clerical walking-out suit and gleaming dog-collar, presiding over a collection of the holy, the halt and the homosexual, Smees among them, pining for Mother Imelda — and all of them lolling back in their chairs and jawing with loud, pink confidence. Kenny was watching with big eyes as Yannovitch puffed away at one of his reeking Abdullah fags. I knew, we all knew, he'd be too frightened to do anything about it. All the same it seemed like tempting fate, what with Gebhardt's warning. And I didn't want anything to go wrong that night. Little Darlin' caught my eye and gave me a wave so wet he might have been sprinkling holy water. There would be others watching us, I knew that.

"It's rather like watching a rehearsal for the Last Supper," Shuckel said.

Yannovitch was the first to go outside not giving a damn who knew it, wandering off the dance floor arm in arm with Rochelle, quite openly peering down her dress and cracking jokes and she shouting delightedly, "Oh Jeez!" and "God, you filthy chap!" and shrieking so she went quite bandy-legged, teetering on her silver high heels with Yannovitch deliberately stopping as they reached the door and turning and flashing a little gold tin of *Crêpe de Chine* French letters he held cupped in his palm. Jack Wyner tried to be more discreet by sending Miss Kingsmead out ahead of him and then ruined his plan by panicking in case he couldn't find her in the darkness and rushing after her woofing and dribbling. Dottie didn't go anywhere. She grabbed van Dam and wouldn't be budged while she told him about the novel she was reading, the story of the Prime Minister's love child who turned out to be coloured and so vastly shamed its parents, they sent it to a special school and visited it at night in a closed car and all went quite well until one day when the boy was grown up he met and fell in love with a ballet dancer little knowing, poor guy, that she was the daughter of the Prime Minister and his very own sister . . .

Judging by the signs, Shuckel and Mina had a short, savage walk in the dark.

He slipped into the seat beside me looking slightly embarrassed. His collar and neck were streaked with red.

"Where's Mina?"

"In the ladies, repairing the damage. My God — what a tiger!"

"Tigress, actually. Was she kissing you or biting you? There's blood on your collar."

He felt for it tenderly. "Marvellous! I'll never wash it off."

"You must have opened her old hockey wound."

He gave a satisfied nod. "Quite possibly. I was working at very close quarters. Are you taking the Smithson outside? No Brothers around. I kept a look-out for the usual posse. Not a sign. They really have kept away."

When Mina came back to the table I saw I had been right. She was dabbing at her lip with a handkerchief. The flesh had opened cleanly, and the horizontal cut showed two rosy, fleshy lips of its own in a tiny, secret smile the rest of her face knew nothing about.

"I can't stand your hair. Why does it lie like that . . . as if it died, or something?" The secret smile gleamed wetly in her lower lip though her face was fierce and tense and registered something I think I'd known since the terrible day on which I'd exposed myself in front of her at Jack Wyner's swimming pool. She hated me. "It's such a personal thing, hair. You sort of associate it with a person, don't you. It's part of them — like the funny crinkly hair of the natives. They say the natives have this little pad of water between the scalp and skull that acts like the cool bag you hang on the car radiator going through the Karoo."

"Perhaps you shouldn't talk too much," Mary said sweetly. "Your poor lip has opened again." She turned to me. "You haven't given me a dance yet, Harry."

"Harry can't dance," Mina said, dabbing away furiously at her lip.

"I think you're bleeding on your teeth," Mary said.

Yannovitch pulled a packet of cigarettes from his pocket and offered me one. When I refused he tucked it behind my ear. "For later . . ."

"You idiot," van Dam sneered, "those are Abdullah you've got there. Donally says Abdullah contain hashish."

"Donally has rocks in his head. These are plain ordinary

smokes, just a little scented, that's all."

He lit up and blew out thick, pungent smoke. People at the tables near us began giving loud stagy sniffs and shouting "Phew!" and "Camel dung!"

Van Dam groaned and buried his head in his arms. "God, oh God! You're making me feel spare. You're just asking for trouble you dumb ape. God, I could die!"

"So die," Yannovitch said. He sent the silver hipflask around the table again.

After the way Mary had dealt with Mina I had to dance with her, of course. I wanted to dance with her. If for no other reason than showing a decent gratitude I proffered the old arm and we waded into the swirling dancers.

"Do you think you might be coloured?"

The question winded me and I couldn't answer. Besides I'd entered the dance against the flow of the tide and we were being badly buffeted. I might say that I began sinking soon after entering the water. Mary turned to me confidently enough to begin with but we were out of our depth in the packed floor moving at speed. My head swam from the vodka.

Out on the floor there was a heavy swell rolling, currents I could not fathom, and I was in over my head before I knew it. Each time I tried to assert myself we'd be swept away by a cannoning backside or knocked sideways by a careering hip. I did not merely stand on Mary's feet; reduced to treading water, as it were, and quickly exhausted, I rested on them for long moments. I felt from the navel downwards the pain I was inflicting on her ankles and saw, in 3-D and technicolour, on a terrible cinema screen inside my skull, each livid smear of polish I left on her pretty blue satin shoes. I lost control about then, broke down completely and began hissing at passing couples and lunging out with my elbow which they thought very funny and danced nimbly away, and Mary was whispering in my ear, "Take it easy, Harry. Just relax and hang on," and she pushed forward bravely on her lap of pain. We'd made it half way around the hall and I saw the doors coming up. I felt her tightening her grip, making subtle shifts of her body so as to adjust my centre of gravity and then bearing up quite wonderfully beneath my floundering weight she lead me backwards, my head lolling stupidly on her shoulder, rather heavily balanced on one breast, whispering encouragement and smiling all the while as she paddled me into the shallows of the foyer beyond the exit doors and, without pausing, out into the warm satin darkness beyond the lights of the hall. I saw the mountainous black of the school buildings, the tarred tennis courts looking wet in the faint moonlight. I had a fit of coughing and she banged me on the back until it passed.

"You're not the world's greatest dancer, Harry."

"I'm no Arthur Murray, certainly."

"It's my fault for dragging you on the floor."

"You deserve a medal. I'm the sorry one. For your shoes. Your feet. For everything. I trained up, you see. But I never got the hang of it. I've been dreading this dance. Scared stiff. Thanks for pulling me out."

She shook her head. "I don't believe you're frightened of anything."

"I have this natural talent for giving the wrong impression. And you? What frightens you most?" Our lips were close and we were talking into each other's mouths.

She thought for a moment and very quietly said: "Rape." The soft explosive little p-sound rippled off my nose. "Not that I thought it up. It's this mad notion of my father's. He's absolutely convinced it's only a matter of time before I'm raped. In his book every African in the country is in the running. He's been convinced since I was about ten. I think he must have convinced me. Sometimes I feel I'm being groomed for the part." She laughed shakily. "And now you. Have you got a terrible fear — besides your colour, that is, or your hair . . . or dancing?"

I thought of all I owed her and so I told her about my breasts.

Her eyes sparkled. "Oh Harry, what nonsense. And anyway I'd have noticed. We've been swimming together, remember?"

"I hide them. Under the ends of my towel. By crossing my arms. And by sunbathing only on my stomach. They're there, I'm telling you. All the guys at school have seen them. You ask anybody. It's a national joke."

"Wait here. I'll be back in a minute." She shot back into the hall and came out with her bag and stole. "All right," she said abruptly, "let's find somewhere private and you can show me."

We went around to the back of the hall.

I knew the stage door would have been left open for Hennie Koekemoer and his men. We could hear them thudding through the Hokey Pokey up front. We felt our way through the darkness heavy with sweaty perfume the dancers pumped out. There wasn't much dancing time left. I found a dressing-room in a short corridor lit by one bare bulb and closed the door against the electric glare. Moonlight streamed through the window. Mary sighed happily, leaning up against the wall and hugged herself. We nuzzled each other briefly and she found the Abdullah Yannovitch had stuck behind my ear. When I said I had no matches she rattled her bag. I lit up and passed it to her; the thick aromatic smoke creamed in the moonlight.

'I didn't know you smoked."

"Like a chimney," she said calmly. "Now, show me the worst."

I took off my jacket. She helped me with the bow tie, undid my buttons, reaching through the smoke, and slipped a soft hand inside my shirt.

"Well?"

"But Harry, they're not at all. I mean, they're ... *fleshy*, I'll admit that. But they're chests, very definitely chests."

I opened my shirt and turned sideways. "People have commented."

"They don't know any better."

"They've been heard to ask my bra size."

"Look here," she instructed, reaching behind her neck where the thin strap looped in the figure eight and instantly the front of her dress fell forward and she was naked from the waist up. "The bra is sewn in," she explained. Then she lined up next to me — and we stood there like two soldiers on parade, shoulder to shoulder in the moonlight. "And remember, I'm smaller than average. Even so, I've got inches on you." She stood there at attention, breasts out, the moonlight pallid on the nipples. "Inches," she repeated proudly.

I turned her around and kissed her. Pulling her to me, taking one breast in my hand and trembling to feel it astonishingly light and smooth. I remember thinking it gave in the hand like the candy-floss we bought at the amusement park at the Easter Agricultural Show. Candy floss in its tissue paper. I was suddenly hungry. I sniffed the breast, I licked it. Mary arched her back and sighed in my hair. Our bare skins pressed together turned moist and stuck. Her kiss was whole-hearted and experienced, judging by the depth and wet clash of it. I responded in the space available using my tongue like a dentist's probe, releasing her breast and pulling her more tightly to me. She responded fiercely, pushing her thigh against me and then it was, without in the least expecting it, that I felt myself hardening alarmingly and knew she must be feeling it too because, truth be told, I came up stiff as a handbrake between us.

I tried to pull back, to free my mouth from hers, to apologise, to change the subject, all the time getting harder and harder but she wouldn't let go, her arms tightened around my waist and for a better hold, I suppose, she slipped her hands into the back of my trousers, behind the cummerband. I tried to warn her but my words were lost in her kiss. I heard the pins pop and my trousers dropped like a fast elevator. I only just managed to catch them as they passed my knees.

Today, how I marvel still at the timing of that entry. To be expected at just that second and no other on God's earth before or since, an image of consuming embarrassment, of defenceless nakedness, burnt into that mad brain, a terrible gift, flaring like a sunburst in the dim recesses behind the steel-plated, saucer-smooth forehead; that it should have been just *that* moment in all eternity which, as we are taught, lasts infinitely longer than it takes the wing of a sparrow brushing by the earth once in a millennium to wear away this world, when the door opened oh, no more than eighteen inches, and light, shockingly bright as a camera flash struck us squarely, twinned as we must have looked with our clothes hanging about us, like snakes rising from our sloughed skins. And indeed Mary's violent intake of breath was a long hiss. I felt sad and immensely heavy all of a sudden and without any energy, and wanted more than anything to fall over and die, and indeed might have done so, or fainted at least, had not Mary's sob in my ear roused me.

"Rape," she said. And then again in a more natural voice, "Rape," as if sensing the more ordinary she made it sound the more likely I was to be convinced.

Looking back now (and I do so often), I see that as the moment of her unhinging. Things could never be the same for her again. In an instant she accepted the truth of her father's mad prophecy. In any event, it was then that she pulled away from me into the darkness, I felt the sweat drying cold on my bare chest and everything was over.

From the doorway, the figure, black with all the light behind it, spoke: "Jesus, Mary and Joseph!" Loud sniffs followed. "What's this? Can it be what I'm thinking? Holy Mother of Mercy! Hashish!"

In the silence that followed I heard it: the soft, sucking sound of a giant slug feeding, rolling a white slurping belly over what it ate, and I knew who stood in the darkness behind this black figure chewing excitedly at his lip. Goble had struck back.

That was the end for me. Something cracked. Tightening my grip on my trousers I made a stumbling, hopping rush at the doorway. Taken by surprise Donally started back crackling brandy fumes. "Get out! Get out!" I slammed the door and leaned against it.

I suppose they could have pushed it open if they'd wanted to but Donally was obviously thinking things over and decided to rest content. They'd seen enough. After a while he spoke through the keyhole. "I'll be going now." His tone was mild. "But you'll not be forgotten."

"Go," I said, "And take Judas with you. And by the way, it wasn't hashish." It seemed important to get that straight.

This brought him back to the keyhole. "Oh, don't you be presuming to tell me, who fought up North at Sidi and Alamein, what is, or is not, hashish — not, if you please, with it raising in my nostrils the same stink as ever it did in the bazaars of Alex."

I listened to him walking away. A jaunty step. Hennie Koekemoer's Trio was banging through "Auld Lang Syne". The dance was over.

I found Mary huddled in a corner, dressed and shaking. She helped me with my tie and her eyelashes brushed my cheek, a sad and gentle touch, like a goodbye wave. It was enormously depressing to see her with her clothes on — as if she'd gone under cover and I'd never see her again as she really was.

"I don't think I could face anyone now."

"No need. I think the taxi will be waiting."

We found the cabbie smoking at the wheel and reading a copy of *True Detective*. "Oi, oi," he said, "sneaking away early. Where will it be, my old mate? The woods? The lake . . .? " He gave me a wink, showing an eyelid thick with reptilian folds.

I ignored him and settled Mary. She pressed her face to my chest and snuffled into my lapel. "Who was it, Harry?"

I knew the driver was listening but I hadn't it in me to care. "Old Donally. The madman. He's been gunning for me. Don't you worry, though. I don't think he'd have recognised you."

"What will he do?"

"He'll think of something."

"I'm sorry I said what I did. But when he burst in like that, I was terrified. I suppose I thought, well, I thought — you know — what my father thinks . . ." She made a big effort, took my arm and squeezed it. "I don't care. Really. We're not at school any more. What can he do? We're free."

" 'Sright," the driver agreed. "Free, white and over twenty-one."

I felt sick. I knew she was frightened. Worst of all, I knew why she was frightened. It wasn't Donally. He had only been the trigger. For the first time she had begun to believe in the dark forces. The cabbie was wrong, at least as far as I was concerned, on all three points.

"Shut up and drive," I said.

Every light in the house was on when I arrived home. The damn place was lit up like a road-house. After paying the fare I had exactly a pound left. If I was going anywhere I knew it wouldn't be far. "Looks like someone's having a party," the driver said.

"Oh, yes," I said carefully. "We're gay dogs here."

"After midnight and still going strong. Terrific!" he said admiringly. "Some folk really know how to live."

My father was out with the roller spiking the lawn. The

reluctant shale gave way with a soft, popping tearing sound beneath the sharp teeth. He saw me and ran into the house emerging with a walking stick and began knocking the heads off the dahlias. When I reached the front door he flung the stick aside with a clatter on the path and raced after me. Inside I found my mother lying face down on the sofa, weeping.

"We know all about you," my father yelled, bouncing me out of the way and going over to stand beside my mother, "and your so-called dance, and your kafoofling, to put it no more strongly, your canoodling and carryings-on with this girl, correction, for all I know, *so-called* girl, as she would have been when you'd finished with her — " and he stormed around the room pulling the antimacassars off the backs of the chairs, crushing them in his hands, biting at their corners and hurling them onto the floor. "This girl, sorry, woman, *fancy-pants* woman, I should have said, unclothed to the waist, to the *waist* — " he banged his hips, " — with her . . ." he lifted his hands to his chest and made shaky passes there like a bad juggler ". . . I won't say what was bared, to spare your mother, not that you'd mind. Oh no. But with her completely naked up here while you fondled and worse and smoked — hashish!"

My mother wailed into the cushions. "Oh Harry, Harry, what lusts have you given way to? And when I think of what a nice, shy child you were!"

"It wasn't hashish," I said stupidly. "It was a cigarette. An ordinary cigarette."

"And did you drink Harry — did you drink too? Tell me the worst," my mother implored.

"Of course he drank," my father yelled, "we've had it from the horse's mouth. Oh yes. We were just off to bed, see. I'd made your mother a cup of tea when there's a knock. That's very late, Molly, I said to your mother. Who'd be visiting at this hour? Don't you ever remember anything, Graham, says she, it's Harry of course, back from his dance, ready to apologise for what he did to his hair. Off I go to the door and who do you suppose I find on the step, but your teacher, the fellow with the shell in his head, dog-collar and all, twirling his rosary beads and his face jumping about like a bioscope. Well, you know me, nothing if not polite: 'Good evening to you Brother,' I say. 'I wish to God it were, Mr Moto', comes the reply. And then he lets me have it. Straight talking. Man to man. No argy bargy. Names, times, witnesses. That's when I placed this girl, no, woman, you were with tonight. I know who she was." He stopped in the middle of the room and lifted up his clenched fists. "You were caught with your pants down, fondling Smithy Smithson's daughter, a man I fought with up North, a powerful man, a client of mine. He'll cancel his policy when he hears. Dammit, he'll sue! Interfering with a minor, that's a crime. You'll have to marry her and she's under age. It'll mean going to court to get permission!"

My mother sat up and covered her ears. "Must you shout, Graham? Must you rant and rave?" she screamed. "Things are bad enough without your broadcasting our shame to the whole neighbourhood." And she fell back on the sofa with her eyes closed.

"There'll be no marriage. Nothing happened. We didn't do anything."

"Won't marry her?" My old man stared. "Well, in that case, expect paternity suits. I know about these things. They'll be here taking tests. Men in white coats with a little bottle for you to make a specimen in. I never thought I'd say this about my own son, but you're a bad risk, Harry. Know what that means? Suppose somebody approached me for cover on you? Insure that, I'd say? I wouldn't touch it with a barge-pole. Not me, no siree!"

My mother stared at me as if across a wide road with great trucks roaring between us. Her eyes were dark, the pupils black, sunk in watery blue; round, little stones drowned in a swimming pool. "Did you think of us — for one moment, Harry, when you were interfering with this girl and smoking drugs? And you in your father's dress suit, too!"

My father began kicking around the newspapers scattered on the floor. "You'll be splashed all over the papers. They'll show your photo with your name underneath and then who'll have you swim in their hoity toity houses? What'll your foreign friends say then? This is a matter for the police, for the doctors, for the press. They'll have you for drugs, they'll have you for rape and they'll have you for — " He broke off abruptly and swallowed hard. I knew what was on his mind.

"For Heaven's sake, Graham," my mother shrilled, "are you trying to send me mad? Weren't you ever taught to complete your sentences?"

My father was in a quandary. He dare not say what he thought. Then he had an idea. Muttering about the "nigger in the woodpile", he began rummaging through the evening paper throwing the pages over his shoulder. When he found what he was looking for he held it up so I could read the headlines. My mother screamed when she saw it and ran out of the room. SOCIETY MATRON ELOPES WITH GARDEN BOY *I Love Him Says S. Africa's Lady Chatterley* ... My father cleared his throat and read aloud in a clear voice:

Lois Chetwyn-van Jaarsveld, 45, wife of a former mayor, John "Jock" Chetwyn-van Jaarsveld, today admitted before a magistrate at a preliminary hearing under the Immorality Act that she had frequently had relations with the gardener, Christmas Mpanza (30) at their stately Ridge home. Relations had taken place over many months in the garage, the tool-shed and in the Wendy House the Chetwyn-van Jaarsvelds had installed in their garden for their two daughters, Ria (6) and Irene (4). It had been, defending counsel submitted, a mutual passion despite obvious difference in the rank and colour and age of the accused ...

My father shook his head wonderingly. ". . . In the tool-shed!"

Somewhere, I could hear my mother crying. The pages my father had thrown away lay across chairs and carpet like dustcovers. They gave the room the look of a place being packed away, a place soon to be left. He was soon quite caught up in the case. I began to back quietly towards the door. Behind me my father began reading the police constable's evidence. The constable told how, acting on information received, he had found the accused lying on her bed in a state of undress at three in the afternoon. When asked what she was doing there she replied that she was, in her own words, "doing her daily dozen." The constable then tested the bedclothes for body warmth and made a search of the house. The other accused, Mpanza was found hiding behind the cocktail bar. He was also naked. When asked his business he told the constable that he was "polishing the glasses . . ."

It was a fine night with just the hint of a breeze and the heavens, as always in the Southern Hemisphere on a good night, were deep and black and dusted in a thick talcum of stars. In the quiet evening my father's voice pursued me. He had begun to read the case for the prosecution. It didn't matter. I was out.

OUT

7

Around lunchtime on a Friday the Koelietown shoppers are thick on the ground in Melkbos Street and along Sir Herbert Baker Avenue. Even moving at a fair trot it took around ten minutes to cover the mile from Raboobie's Outfitters to Singh's Select Tailors, such were the jostling crowds out for the Eternal Sales and the Unbeatable Bargains. The numbers always grew on Friday, payday, into great continental migrations; Europe met Africa; met, mingled, gathered head and roared into the triangular island that was Asia; ran out foaming over the tiny, glittering streets flooding the dark enticing alleys. You got nowhere pushing against the raging tide and learnt quickly how to skirt the crowds by swinging out into the gutter every so often to pick up speed, jumping the traffic lights and cutting down dank little alleyways heavy with the smell of chappatis, leather and old lettuce leaves.

At Singh's I collected a pair of charcoal pants, cut down from the knee, tapering to eleven-inch stove-pipes, for this trainee bank-teller from Barclays, desperate to dazzle the foyer during the Saturday matinee at the Capital Bioscope or the Opera House Bio-Cafe, hoping to lead some besotted babe down to the passion pit of the one-and-twopence seats. He's seen the charcoals on Raboobie's EVERYTHING MUST GO! ALL-TIME GREAT SALE!!! and bought them to go with his white sportscoat with gold fleck and padded shoulders, picked up on Raboobie's UNDER NEW MANAGEMENT SALE! the month before.

This dumbo had the idea he'd beaten Raboobie down a pound. Meanwhile, Raboobie got those charcoals at a special discount from his Connection who drove up from Durban once a month in his Hudson Hornet with more white fur stretched along the dashboard than you'll see on a polar bear, hot from his factory somewhere on the South Coast packed with starving Indian seamstresses working from patterns stolen from American magazines. Raboobie bought them at two quid, sale-priced them at four, and happily took three. They hung well enough to begin with but the seat showed a shine inside six months. It was a pair of the same van Dam had been good enough to sell to me at the first tell-tale glimmer.

Singh's Select Tailors sat at the northern tip of Koelietown where Sir Herbert Baker Avenue ran into Main Street, pushing a sharp nose into the under-belly of the white city centre. Nearing home just off Melkbos Street and two doors down John X. Merriman Parade I collected from Hassim's Wholesale Drapers a nice, shocking pink shirt for an old ironing girl calling that afternoon. A heavy pair of real leather, black Jarmans, newly steel-tipped for clickety walking, heel and toe, for "Cheeky" Nene, a hot-shot from Queen Mary Location, were ready at Miami Shoe Store owned by the brothers Karim, doing well, this their third branch on a prime site just off Blood Lane. Last on the list was a pair of 32 Levis from Goolam's Gents Outfitters down Gandhi Crescent, on order for none other than old Gino Ferranti, he of the polio-withered arm, my old class-mate, who gave me the fright of my life when he turned up at Raboobie's one day and astonishingly failed to recognise me, looked right through me; an experience that left me shaking and astounded until I remembered the invisible school cleaners of St Bonaventure's; and then I was home again, heading for Raboobie's on Melkbos, a short stubby little street that broke off abruptly, like a snapped pencil, when it came up hard on its west side against the corrugated bulk of the railway marshalling shed. Behind Raboobie's shop lay the simmering, shouting, steaming wilderness of the shunting yards, making the broad immovable base of the magic triangle that was Koelietown.

"I never let the customer know I haven't got what he wants — which is more than often the case. I flog him something else or I get it from another branch. Of course, I haven't any other branches. And then again, every shop in Koelietown is my branch. We compete here, you know, but we don't cut each other's throats. We prefer to bleed the customer. They give us their blood and we give them dreams ... Koelietown is a place of dreams. People come here believing anything can happen. How can we disappoint them? — Poor bastards."

On the night I left home, I came to Raboobie's like a spy to a safe house. His shop in Maharaj Mansions in Melkbos Street was dark and shuttered in steel. The gable unpeeled flakes of paint; they fell like leaves in the moonlight. "Mansions" was putting it strongly. The place managed two squat stories; *Est. 1903* it said boldly on the gable. But the spirit was gone, you felt that. It was my first inkling that here was a place actually working at falling apart. I took a deep breath and went inside, up the rickety staircase under a feeble yellow light and knocked on the door on the first landing. Raboobie was some time coming. He opened the door slowly and stood there rubbing his thick hair, the red stones winking on his ring fingers.

"I've come for Shaligram's job."

He went on rubbing his hair with one hand. With the other he absent-mindedly felt the cloth of the lapel of my dress suit. "Good stuff."

"It's Savile Row."

Without another word he led me up the next flight of stairs, opened a door and left without a word. This was my bedroom. The only window in the room was papered over with old, sun-bleached newspaper that crackled as I opened it. I looked down on black steam engines massively quiet now, past midnight, and faintly gleaming among webs of track. The room had in it a bed with blankets but no sheets, a table and chair. There was not another thing there. I knew because I looked very carefully. Then I lay down on the bed and went to sleep. I had never been so happy in my life.

I was woken by the room shaking as if it were going somewhere and the yells of the shunters. Puffs of steam drifted past my window and vanished into the blue sky. In the passage I found a jaundiced lavatory and wash basin. In the mottled mirror I saw my face covered with smuts from the engines. The window would have to stay closed at night. I washed and went downstairs.

Raboobie's big display window was the most beautiful in Melkbos Street, squared off in bright red paper, framing the bargains of the century, everything you ever wanted to buy at PRICES SLASHED BEYOND BELIEF!!! A lovely sight. I never tired of coming home to the good news lettered in acid-green lightning bolts zig-zagging around the red border, eyeball-bouncing stuff: SALE! SALE! SALE! "Final Clearance" it was that week. To every season its sale: "Fire-damage" and "Bankruptcy", "The Queen's Birthday", "Under New Management", "Christmas", "Easter", "Father's Day", and "Day of the Covenant" and, in between, "Half-Price Sales", "Closing-Down Sales", "Grand Re-Opening Sales", finally dwindling, in the low time of the year when Raboobie took his holidays just after the "January Sales" and a cousin ran the shop, to small events like "The Sale of the Century" and the "Sale of Sales", while he paddled his toes in the Indian Ocean writing his poetry nobody wanted, at a little place near Winkelspruit owned by his mother's cousin's brother, one Kasim Baba, "a good Durban boy, very big in suits down Grey Street way." That window was all life's feast to me.

Black, white, khaki and powder-blue jeans saddle-stitched in red, laced with gold and silver zips. Shirts green, pink, white and striking mauve, broad collars and button-holes picked out in beige or blue, bold monograms above breast pockets, and at the neck, instead of a button-hole a cunning hook of plaited black cotton to take the top button lying snug under the fat Windsor knot of your Slim Jim tie. Candy-striped socks flashier than barber's poles, elasticised skin-huggers so thin your ankles gleamed in them like traffic lights, luminous orange and shocking pink. In corners of the window there lay like weird entrails great tangles of string ties; red, yellow, two-tone purple and white, ends nipped in brass and silver caps and caught in oval brass discs with initials, used for drawing the string tie around the neck in an adjustable noose. And behind all that, to me the best of all, climbing to the back wall of the window in shining racks, reposing on crushed velvet, the sort you see only in open coffins and new watch-boxes, nestling in baby-blue softness, gleaming under the neon and cunningly worked up with tissue in the toes, were row on row of shoes: brilliantly liquid patent leathers, heavy Jarmans like broad, black duckfeet, winkle-pickers pointing Turkish slipper toes, Indian Moccasins looped with bows or pom-poms or knotted leather thongs, soft suedes in deep rich blue and brown, and casual Italian leather step-ins, bossed with silver buckles and speckled with exotic perforations.

The doorway was hung with suits and jackets, maroon, midnite blue, off-off white, hairy green, biscuit, chequer board, salt and pepper and houndstooth all with blood-bright linings, the shoulders stiffly padded and cut long to reach the knee and split behind to the waist by a single vent. BUY 1 SUIT — GET 3 PANTS FREE!!! and BUY 5 SHIRTS — GET 1 JACKET FREE!! The placards flapped above the lintel. A loudspeaker broadcast to the passing street the continuous refrain interspersed with fanfares of electric guitars, penny-whistles and sitars. Beside the loudspeakers, in brass letters which I polished every morning, were displayed his titles and licence number registered under the Trading Act: *Kasiprasad Raboobie, Owner & Sole Prop.*, Maharaj Mansions, 146c, Melkbos Street.

"My very dear sir, I have your beautiful trousers." Raboobie took the parcel from me, slit the cellophane with a thumbnail grown for the purpose and especially manicured, and folded back the brown paper in one blurred movement. The char-coals, neatly pressed, lay marvellously over his wrists and he was offering them to the customer, the Barclays bank teller, at the same time pointing him with his elbow towards the changing room at the back of the shop. "You'll find a hanger in there, dear sir. Off with the old and on with the new and give us the pleasure of a good look at the superb fit."

We listened to him grunting behind the plywood partition, banging his elbows as he struggled to change in the two-foot-square box.

Most of Raboobie's customers were white. He had a trickle of Indian trade, and a fair turnover in a couple of special lines for Africans: blankets, tin chests and shiny leather shopping bags along with pink shirts, for some reason especially popular with washerwomen. There came too, special cus-tomers from the Queen Mary Location. You got to know them soon enough. "What can I do?" Raboobie would ask.

"They're a lot of bloody hoods. But do they not pay? We do business. We don't talk about the weather."

Tweetie Boy Molefe came to Raboobie's in those days. And Daddy Long Legs Kunene of the Shebeens, splendid in golf shoes and white panama. And the axe man, "Cheeky" Nene; Walter Zulu, the bicycle spoke boy, blind in one eye and breathing strangely; and Babyface Dumile, the child killer, full of smiles, bashful and on his shaven skull a gleam dancing towards the crown. And, of course, all their back-up crews came too, propping up the walls, in jeans and dark glasses, chewing on matchsticks and picking their noses. For them he kept Fedoras, Panamas, black shirts and silver ties, shiny blue suits with wide lapels, two-tone golf shoes, spats and canes. They bought what they saw Mad Dog Coll and Lucky Luciano wearing in the old gangster movies they gate-crashed on Saturday nights at the Bantu Men's Social Club in the Location. Christ knows their buying methods were anything but subtle. A flash suit, a Homburg, a belted coat — they'd point, pay and go.

"That's O.K. by me. I'm not marrying into their families," Raboobie told me. "I'm reserving my kindness, man, for the good people who pass my door. But I don't waste my time with these criminals who're going to end up one Monday morning hanged by the neck until they're dead in Pretoria Central. I sell, they buy. Like the government, I don't believe in boycotts. But I have relations only with proper humans."

Raboobie lounging in the doorway of his shop under his brass name-plate, the bicycle shop music blaring, half hidden among the sports jackets hanging left and right, watching the passing trade, threw out smiles like fishhooks and reeled in the wriggling customers. It was an honour to watch him work over a potential buyer, taking the lapel of his jacket between thumb and forefinger, his plump face honest, thoughtful, rubbing the cloth with his smile disappearing the way chalk does off a blackboard, bit by bit until only the traces stay: "Man! Where d'you buy this? Let me tell you, sir — you won't think I'm rude, sir? — I must tell you, this cloth, it's no good. Listen my friend, come inside. I got some lovely stuff. Top quality. Straight from America only this morning. You don't have to buy. Costs nothing to look." Raboobie could undress a man in about two minutes flat, no offence intended, and tog him out again. "Never mind the price, we're not talking money now, sir. You're just looking, right? Now, that jacket you got on there, dear sir, go on, look in the mirror, feel it, go on *feel*, sir, isn't that quality cloth? Straight from America, limited shipment, just like they show in *Jailhouse Rock*, sir, you go to the bioscope? Yes? Then you know, I don't have to tell you what you're wearing now is a one-hundred-per-cent-genuine-Elvis-Presley-jacket   . . ."   He switched styles, clothes, whole wardrobes like a magician forcing cards, going by a flicker in the prospect's eyes for signs he was on the right track, moving easily from khaki jeans (a non-starter) into a beautiful pair of dove-gray slacks, guaranteed 100 per-cent genuine wool. As-Worn-By-Tab-Hunter (better, but not quite there yet), to something very, *very* special, last pair left, reserved for another customer, but what can one do if he isn't here? Absolutely the latest line in charcoal slacks, newest American leisure-wear, guaranteed never to wrinkle or shine. (Beautiful!) "Look sir yourself, the mirror does not lie, as the saying goes. Magnificent line in the leg. Don't worry about the seat being a bit loose, it's the cut sir, the boy will run for us to the tailor . . . Harry!"

Koelietown wasn't where I'd aimed for the night I'd left home. I walked blind for a long time and somehow came to rest in the small hours outside Singh's Select Tailors who were having their "Slightly Shopsoiled Sale!!! BUY ONE SUIT — GET SIX TIES, TWO BELTS FOUR SOX — FREE!!" Without realising it, I'd crossed into Koelietown. Main Street with its big office blocks and Central Police Station, heart of the white city centre, was the boundary. But the White suburbs faded so quickly, bit by bit, slow as Raboobie's smile when he fingered bad cloth in a customer's lapel, that unless you were careful you could be across the border and into Indian country before you knew it. On the hoardings outside the Delhi Cinema were splashed the forthcoming attractions. There was this film starring Shashi Kapoor, I remember, and about a dozen women, all with very red lips and purple eyes, and the way they were looking at him I got the feeling he treated them badly.

The pride of Barclays Bank came out of the changing room trying to peer over his left shoulder at the cut of the charcoals across his backside, at the same time pulling worriedly at his crotch. The eleven-inch bottoms of his tapered trousers clamped around his ankles like crab claws.

Raboobie clapped his hands in delight. "Perfect, my dear sir! But come over here and let us admire you properly. How superb!" Effortlessly he turned the clerk this way and that as if he were handling a suit on a hanger.

"Jeez, you really think so, hey?" Swaying like a man on a narrow ledge he craned his neck to see behind him how the trousers held his calves.

"Positively a beautiful line in the leg. Here, let me show you." Raboobie clicked his fingers. "Harry, mirror for the boss."

In the eighteen months I stayed with Raboobie he kept his nose out of my business. We agreed on the story that I was from Port Elizabeth way, a place neither of us knew at all, and just passing through. Noticing that I avoided the cops, he asked me if they were after me and when I said they might be, slapped me on the shoulder. "Buck up," he said, "aren't they after everybody?" Then, too, he wondered quite openly about the look of me.

"With that hair you don't pass for an Indian. A coloured, is that what you are, hey? A Malay? They got coloureds in Port Elizabeth, Harry? There is a touch of tar in you, I can see that. Yet you could pass for a white at a pinch. Jolly puzzling."

"Let's just say I'm some kind of kaffir, and leave it at that. O.K.?"

"O.K. by me. But I don't like that word, man. Mixed blood?"

"My blood's all right. Skin's the problem. Say a *white* kaffir, then . . ."

"Well, I suppose you mean as opposed to a Bantu, a non-white, an African, a native, or an ordinary common-or-garden kaffir?"

"As opposed to everything, actually."

That really amused him and he laughed until the sweat hung from his eyebrows.

He was good-humoured like that always — until what he called the dejections came in from the magazines. "You wouldn't believe it, Harry. Thirty times I have sent my poems to *The Outspan*. Thirty times they've said to me — "Take them away, please." He showed me a stack of differently coloured slips of paper — his dejections. "Here — listen to this:

Far in Afric's burning veldt
Next the brilliant sea
Faintly is my love's name spelt
On the lone thorn tree . . ."

His eyes got all watery and he sort of choked over the last few words. "This poem means very much to me," he touched his heart, "it celebrates my tragic loss."

"Gosh, I'm sorry, Mr Raboobie. I mean, I don't know anything about poetry except maybe — *A garden is a lovesome thing, God wot* . . . which I learnt at school. That sounds very sad. Were you married?"

"Not married, betrothed! Betrothed and bereaved in a week. Meningitis. Very fatal. I was here, planning the Easter Sales. She was in Durban, preparing to join me. We were to marry in Balfour where her family had their place. Suddenly all was nothing."

"Do you send in your stuff to the magazines under your own name?"

"But of course."

"I only asked because — look, don't get me wrong but yours is a very, well, *Indian* name and, you know, these magazines, they probably say to themselves when your poems pop through the letter box, 'Christ, it's that koelie again!' "

"But my name is Kasiprasad Raboobie! I stand in the long line of Bengali poets writing in the language of the British Empire. My father was the friend of Manmohan Ghose. On my mother's side I am related to the great Dutt family, poets all! Should I call myself van der Westhuizen, or Groenewald?" He spat through the doorway.

But late at night he'd blub his eyes out so that the upper floor of Maharaj Mansions, cheap boxwood that it was, shook with the force of it and I'd wake thinking it must be morning and the engines shunting in the yard below.

The bank teller grabbed at his fly, shifting from leg to leg.

"It feels damn tight in the crotch."

I hung about in the doorway. Raboobie was on his knees fiddling between the clerk's thighs with the tape measure.

"Absolutely not," he announced. "Cut by our master tailor to suit you wonderfully, sir, these charcoals. What we call in the trade a snug fit. There's meant to be a slight bulge in front — that's the fashion. But if you're not happy, do me a favour sir, and ask your wife what she thinks."

"Wife!" The clerk had a laugh like an angry Alsatian. "Do I look bloody stupid? I'm a bachelor. To drink the milk you don't have to marry the cow."

"You've got a jolly fine sense of humour, sir." Raboobie didn't laugh.

After he'd changed back into his grey safari shirt, obviously feeling pretty pleased with himself, the clerk leaned on the counter and stared at me while Raboobie wrapped the trousers.

"Who's he?" He jerked a thumb.

"That's my runner. A clever boy. His name's Harry."

"He isn't Indian. Not dark enough."

"Eurasian. That's a boy of mixed parentage, you know."

"I know what's Eurasian — another name for coloured, hey? That's why they got the Immorality Act — it's against this racial mixing. You get albinos otherwise," the clerk said flatly. "Funny hair, too."

Raboobie kept his eyes on his work. "He is from P.E. way."

For some reason the clerk thought this incredibly funny. He held on to his bruised crotch and fell about laughing.

After a while Raboobie joined in. So did I. What the hell — I laughed at worse things when I was a runner for Raboobie.

106

8

My previous life became something I trailed around with me and which I tried not to think of, something like a withered arm as thin and bony as old Gino Ferranti's, who sat in front of me in class at St Bonaventure's. Wrapped in his shirt sleeve, you didn't know it was there except when the wind flapped the sleeve. Once, during the polio epidemic, when Brother Donally asked who hadn't had their injections, Gino stuck up that arm. For a joke! Just so it was that I hid the dragging mutilation of my past. I didn't care to touch it to see if there was any feeling left. The mind may well have windows (always Donally's big line in his Catechism classes . . .) or was it Soul? I'm not sure. Anyway, whatever — mine had curtains. And I kept them drawn. Not back nor forward did I look. No sir! It was enough to be moving between Melkbos and Main with a pair of herring-bone slacks and two pairs of Levis under my arm wrapped in brown paper. I didn't care where I was heading — after that. In my opinion people are too damn confident about the future. Just like they are about "overseas". Who's to say that any such things exist? I've seen no signs.

Raboobie and I were talking politics one slack Thursday, standing between the jackets in the doorway of his shop, taking the sun, watching the street. Raboobie was going on about old Gandhi, who, it seems, was once in very big with the Indian traders, to begin with at least, when he first came to this country. Raboobie was gloomy. The way he saw it, race relations were at rock bottom. The only people who hated Asians worse than the whites did, he said, were the blacks. Things were getting so bad that if the government chartered a big boat and packed the Indians back home the whole country would turn up on the quay to wave goodbye. They'd even club together to pay the Lady in White to sing them out of sight just as she did the troopships in the war.

"This is bloody silly thinking, Harry, I'm telling you. We Indians aren't White. We aren't playing for the *apartheid* side. Though to see how some Indians behave you wouldn't think so. We'd better improve our manners pretty damn quickly and stand together with the non-Whites or end up on our bums. Passive resistance — you heard of that Harry? Now, there's the way! We ought to follow the Mahatma's teachings. All of us, Indians, Africans, coloureds together, we should move into the white city centre one fine morning just about the time all the masters and madams are driving to their offices and lie down in the middle of the road."

"Then what?"

"And then nothing, Harry. This is passive resistance, see. No violence is Gandhi's way. We stay there a couple of hours maybe. We stop them, we make them reconsider."

"Excuse me, Mr Raboobie, but what's to reconsider? They'll just drive their Jags and Pontiacs slap over you. Without even noticing, could be. No hard feelings, right. Ooops! Sorry! Didn't see you lying there, ahem. Around five in the afternoon, they'd drive back home again after work. Squelch! A second time. Then the municipal sweepers will come along with brooms and hoses and wash your blood and guts down the stormwater drains so the whole place is tidy again for the next day."

Raboobie chewed his lip thoughtfully. "Harry, I think you're too young, old chap, to understand politics. Unless we non-whites become brothers, unless we make a stand, like General Custer, y'know, we'll all go down the drain anyway. Look at the city over there, Harry."

I looked. The skyscrapers rose up out of the smudgy heat haze, packed against the blue sky.

"The white city grows taller," Raboobie said softly, "and fatter. The more it has, the more it wants. It's hungry and looks to see what next it may eat. The white suburbs lie all around, but it cannot eat its own. It looks down, and there on its own doorstep it sees who sitting there — but ourselves? And it grabs us. The whites want us out of Koelietown. But for us there are only two ways out of Koelietown — " he jerked a thumb over his shoulder towards the marshalling yards behind his shop — "under the wheels of a train, or — " he lifted his chin in the direction of John X. Merriman Street and the cemetery — "or they plant us six feet under the green gravel stones. All land within fifty yards of the marshalling sheds is Government property. Melkbos Street is the first that must go. The land stretching from the railway tracks to the other pavement over there belongs to the South African Railways. The Government has re-zoned it as a white business area and bought it from the SAR for a tickey, or something nominal like that. So we have to get out."

Across the road I could see the fahfee agents collecting stakes. At the end of the street the fahfee man himself sat in the back of his bottlegreen Chev, the thin Chinese mouth making a third blind eye beneath his dark glasses. "I've got to move out, Harry, man. It breaks my heart. But I can't wait here in Maharaj Mansions until they serve an eviction order. It could be tomorrow or next year. I've known it a long time. I'm moving before they move me. I thought you ought to know."

"But where will you go?" I felt hollow, as if I hadn't eaten for days.

"Where will *you* go, Harry? That's the question, as Hamlet says. Me, I'll set up shop again — what'd you expect? I got an option on a lease on a place higher up near Blood Lane, owned by a cousin of the Goolam Brothers. Nice bit of frontage. But no rooms to rent, you understand Harry? No space. The crowding is bad already in Koelietown. Now we're going to have to make even less of ourselves. I'm not throwing you out, Harry. You can stay here in the room until I go, have no fear about that."

"When are you off?"

He whistled through his teeth and watched the fahfee collectors sticking the money into canvas bags. "End of the month. But come, Harry, cheer up. Look, the Chinaman's collecting the fahfee money. Let me take a ticket for you. Perhaps I'll win your fortune. What do you dream at night? Tell me your dream and they'll give you a number."

"I don't have dreams."

"Come on, you could win a hundred pounds."

"What will I do with a hundred pounds — put it away for my funeral?"

He brightened. "Funerals! That's more like it. They'll have a wide selection of numbers. Rely on me. I'll choose one that suits you to a T."

Mama, the fruit-seller, worked her pitch by the railway bridge beneath the great clanging steps the workers shoved their way down on their way to the offices and factories. Soon after four each morning they arrived on the trains. After four each afternoon they fought their way up the stairs again, leaving the city centre to its empty streets where the only moving thing was, sometimes, an escaped newspaper flinging itself around a lamp-post. Listen — they say that after the bomb fell on Hiroshima there was this terrible silence. Well, you can hear the same silence in the white city centre after six p.m. every day of the week.

Why did they run and shove like that? Search me. You'd think they were after prizes, or something. Once, on British Movietone News, I saw this newsreel of Italian crowds waiting to greet the Pope outside St Peter's. His Holiness was going to come out and bless them. Only he doesn't come out of the door he is expected to, he comes out on the other side, at the top of some steps. These Italians spot him and run like crazy up these steps, falling, some of 'em biting their hankies, crying and tearing their hair. But I knew it couldn't have been the Pope who caused this excitement down at the railway station every morning and evening. Not the Pope. Not in Koelietown, no.

Mama, yes, she was always there by the steel stairs, from first light to last, filling small, square, brown-paper packets with oranges, naartjies, mottled, softening bananas, grapes small and white as blisters. Mama herself, though she took what shade the steps offered, burnt in the unchanging, inexhaustible, idiot African sun a dark purple with a heavy bloom to her skin like the last plum in a packet. When it rained and muddy rivers cut through the red dusty approaches to the station she moved her stall right under the steel stairs and the workers pouring up and down over her head made a humble umbrella and kept her dry.

Not long after the bank teller bought his charcoals too

110

tight in the crotch and Raboobie talked about evictions, Mama called to me as I passed her pitch on my way back to the shop carrying from Miami Shoes a pair of tan Tom-Toms for an articled clerk with a lisp.

"What, Runner-Like-The-Wind! Today, you are slower than the tok-tokkie."

"Today my heart is heavy, Mama. The Indians are going from Melkbos Street. The white men are coming to live there. I can run no longer."

She nodded contentedly and stuck up eight fingers. "Domkop! You tell Mama nothing. For so many years I have known the White men were coming to chase the Koelies." She did a little dance kicking the air. " 'Voetsak! Voetsak!' the white man says. And the Koelies hear them and go like this." Mama ran on the spot. "It is good. You are a man now. Running is for boys, Mama knows. You must find a wife." She filled up the packet with oranges and plums. "No, no, leave your money, Runner-Like-The-Wind. This is the last fruit. If we do not eat it, it goes vrot."

"But I have money. Even the last fruit should be paid for."

"So — you are a rich man! Good. Buy a wife, then. Your father and mother they sit at home. Listen!" She cocked an ear. She hugged her breast and sobbed. "They cry — 'Oh why has our son no wife, no sons?' Think of your mama."

"But you are my mama."

Her lips let go their puckerings and stretched smiling across pink gums. "Ai ai ai! Such a cheekiness to one so old! You could be the son of the son of my youngest child. Run! Or the white man is there in Melkbos before you."

Sometimes I thought about my mother. I felt I should set her mind at rest. Perhaps a phone call. I got as far as the tickey box on the corner of John X. Merriman but stopped at the first digit. What was I to say? She'd cry and want to know what I was doing. When I explained I was a runner for Raboobie in Koelietown she'd break down. When she told my father, he'd lose his temper, hop around on one leg slapping his knee. When Charity found out she was working for a family of coloureds, some of whom were working for Indians, life wouldn't be worth living. When the neighbours heard how young Harry had gone native they'd sell the story to the newspapers. So I wrote this letter instead:

Dear Mom — You'll be pleased to know that my chest is responding to treatment (i.e. my breathing exercises, remember?) I'm growing hair there, too. It all helps! No such luck with my arches. But never mind, you can't win them all, as they say. I'm also putting on weight. I will come and see you one day when all this has "blown over". In the meantime DON'T WORRY. I am quite O.K.

Harry.

P.S. Give my regards to Charity.

I put in the bit about Charity to show her I wasn't sulking, and got Raboobie's charcoal pants connection to post it from Durban.

9

It was at Raboobie's that I first met Koosie who was to do much to further my career; who sent me to University — for the afternoon: car thief, clown, aide, confidante, messenger, musician, joker and fall-guy to the hoods from the Queen Mary Location. Small, dapper, honey-skinned, smelling of Ingram's after-shave, he'd wink at me under his Fedora when I came in with a fine pair of houndstooth trousers from Jhavari Tailors for Daddy Long Legs Kunene, draw me aside into the corner of the shop where soft, fat bales of cloth staggered up to the roof and chat to me of Port Elizabeth and East London of which he knew a great deal having been brought up in New Brighton township. I'm afraid I was a hopeless conversationalist because I knew nothing at all of that part of the world but Koosie was more interested in talking than listening and never noticed, or if he did he was too polite to say so. He was going to be a professional flute player. He only ran with the big men from Queen Mary in an advisory capacity in order to save money he needed for his new life. When he had saved enough, he was going to America; he had a sponsor there, a woman in Galveston, who had promised to put him through music school. He had a secret route ready when the time came to leave the country. He drew a map for me on the back of the cigarette card inside his tin of Mills Cigarettes: Luxury Length. The escape route was known in the trade as the Bechuanaland Jump.

One day Koosie said to me: "Ever been to University, pally?"

I said, "Maybe." In fact in all my time in Koelietown I'd never been into the White centre. Partly because I'd no wish to go back to the world I'd left. Mainly because I was happy

113

where I was. The only places I'd visited were the shops where I called on my rounds. This was an intellectually limiting existence. The extent of my conversation seldom reached beyond: "I'm the boy from Raboobie's" and "I've come for the alterations."

"You like music?" Koosie asked. "Got a natural sense of rhythm? Fixed up! We'll go to a jazz session. We'll go hear old Julius play. He's a bagful of sweet sounds, that old piano player. And we'll sit back in those plush red seats in that big 'Varsity hall and do our tiny nuts. How about it, Harry? You never had it so good in Port Elizabeth, I'm telling you." He caught the question in my eyes and added: "It's multi-racial up there at the 'Varsity — they mix. Very cool about colour, those bebops. Don't worry about a thing. You come with me. We gotta get you educated. Can't work for Koelies all your life."

Rumour has it that Rome is built on seven hills. Our town almost missed being built on just one. It was called Kitchener's Ridge. When the Nationalist Government took over — in 1948 — the sun set for the last time and a great darkness settled on the land and the name was changed immediately to Triomfrand, though everyone continued to refer to it as the Ridge. In the beginning the first town planners didn't think much of the hill and after they'd planted the fort, the prison and the university up there they forgot all about it. Later the Seminary was added. As the city spread across the plain, some bright spark realised that the further houses were in danger of disappearing over the horizon forty miles away and all the time there was this dirty great mound in the middle of the town just waiting to be built on. The Western Ridge remained suburban, green and gracious and being home to the rich it was protected, a kind of game park of the upper middle classes. The Eastern Ridge was given to the builders. And build they did. Skyscraper offices, hotels, shopping centres went up like rocket ships and hundreds of blocks of flats were built to solve the housing problem. Trouble was that the locals didn't take to inner city, high-rise flat life. No gardens, see? No decent South African feels at home unless he looks out of his picture window across at least half an acre of strong green kikuyu grass all dotted about with sweating garden boys. So, in time, the Eastern Ridge was taken over by European immigrants whom the Government lured to the Union with a free passage and promises that the streets were paved with servants. Before long this skyscraper zoo was packed to the gills with a motley crew of Continentals. There were English fitters and turners who crowded the 1820 Settlers Clubs most evenings raising reedy voices in "Knees Up Mother Brown" and bitching about the local beer and/or the slackness of their cook-girls. There were plenty of Italians, too. Many, it seemed, had been taken prisoner up North in the desert during the war and enjoyed the captive life so much that they'd stayed on to open restaurants with names like Benito's Hideaway and Selassie's Kitchen. And the Germans . . . well, they came after the war and traditionally packed the bierkellers on the anniversary of Hitler's birthday and sang the Horst Wessels song while portly Jews in yarmulkas who'd left Germany to escape just these Germans paraded on the pavements outside carrying placards saying "Gestapo Out" and "Remember Belsen", which, if you ask me, was pretty useless since about half this pig-ignorant country probably thought Gestapo was the soup sold in Spanish kitchens and Belsen was a town in the Orange Free State, and the other half had been rooting for the Germans during the war, anyway. Usually, these evenings ended with the two sides knocking the shit out of each other. The cops would rock up with Alsatians and next morning the papers ran pictures showing guys having their kneecaps eaten under headlines like "Police Dog Kaiser's Bite is Worse than his Bark!" It was on the Eastern Ridge, dwarfed by flats and offices, that the University stood proudly among its parking lots.

Walking through the gates, feeling vulnerable, my collar up as a precaution against recognition, beside a beaming Koosie, wasn't the way I'd expected to go to university. But there you are. Set up high on the eastern edge of the Ridge, at the top of Koffiefontein Drive, the first really impressive thing I noticed about 'Varsity were the thousands of cars; this was a university for motor cars: Alfa Romeos six-deep, teams of Volvos, more TR3s, MGs, more Jags than you'd see in the starting line at Le Mans, roadsters so fancy I'd only seen pictures of them, at least seven varieties of Porsche,

Mercedes like they were going out of fashion, not to mention an entire museum of vintage stuff including a Cord or two, Bentleys for Africa, an old Packard nicely chromed and painted pillar-box red, plus all the usual Fords, Pontiacs and so on. Koosie hummed as we threaded our way through the cars, and he'd pat one that especially caught his eye as if it were a dog that had just done a clever trick. Scrawled in the dust along the sides and windows of some of the cars were strange slogans: *Herod Got A Bad Press, The Queen Keeps Coal in Her Bath, One Man One Vote, Shirley is a Kugel.*

At the university gates a crowd of students carrying placards were holding a demonstration. The placards said things like: CIVIL RIGHTS? BARELY CIVIL — NEVER RIGHT! INTERN VERWOERD! AFRICA FOR THE AFRICANS! and SUPPORT VARSITY RUGBY! It was, Koosie explained, the usual afternoon protest. About twenty yards away, on a traffic island in the middle of the road, a smaller group of students without placards waved their fists and sang songs. These were the Afrikaans students, who opposed the English liberals, holding their usual afternoon counter-protest, Koosie told me. He glanced at both sides in disgust. "These White cats are all crazy. They reckon they're doing something about the politics of the twentieth century, *apartheid* and all that. Meanwhile, they're really still fighting the Boer War." He pointed out how you could tell the different branches of students. The art students one knew by their ponchos, rough woven kaffir-sheeting dyed red and black, draped over sky-blue jeans, Chelsea boots and veld-skoen; medics in crisp white lab coats, multi-coloured ball-points and clip-on combs glinting from breast pockets, standing around trying to look older than everybody else with their Wanderers Club ties and moaning about there never being enough parking at demonstrations; chemists wearing carefully placed acid burns in their lapels; engineers in heavy khaki woollen socks collapsing around their ankles in thick swirls; embryo dentists, smartest of all, in silk shirts of dirty — and hence authentic — cream, confident as head prefects under elaborate Vaseline cowlicks; the crowd darkened here and there by the academic gowns of lonely pedants, aged black garments, in the sunshine glimmering now an oily brown, now a greasy blue-green sheen, with a threadbare swing from the shoulders, cutting nastily into the armpits and falling inches short of the knee; legal clerks and accountants in articles who came straight from work in sober city suits but often got lost on the way, Koosie explained, and so held private meetings in obscure corners of town unmolested by police and public who took them for Jehovah's Witness prayer meetings. The students were blocking the traffic, as per usual, with the motorists rolling down their windows to yell things like, "Go back to Ghana!" and "Bloody homos!" and "Get yourself a haircut!" and the students giving them back embarrassed little salutes, clenched fists raised no higher than their nipples, keeping a sharp eye on the Afrikaans storm-troops massing on the traffic island for another raid, reforming and careering into the English enemy, throwing yellow paint, eggs and monkey nuts, chanting bits of the National Anthem and little known Boereliedjies picked up in remote army camps in South West Africa, whipped on by huge cheerleaders, their blonde heads cropped close as mielie cobs, whom you took for demented lock forwards until you noticed the bibles under their arms and realised they were probably third year Theology students. And the cops watched it all, waiting, spitting on their palms and smacking their truncheons against their calves, fiddling with the press-studs on their holsters, bossed by a colonel with a swagger stick whose belly fought his Sam Browne every inch of the way. The demonstrators kept their clenched fist salutes only nipple high because any higher than that invited trouble since your passing constable might think he was being assaulted and knock the living shit out of his attackers. When that happened the papers would get pictures, naturally, and run them the next morning under a headline NO OFFENCE MEANT! and report that the cop was forced to take action because the silly damn student had insulted his aged mother who was living alone in Westonaria on a widow's pension. In these cases the blood was real enough. Trouble is that in the newspaper pictures it always looked such poor stuff on the pavement, Koosie lamented — it could have been *anything*.

On the outskirts of the demo the usual black crowd gathered: the African messengers in khaki, spilling out of the offices, staring and giggling politely behind their hands, winking at the nannies drawn by magic from the nearest parks and playgrounds with their white kids, cheering first one team then the other and in between finding time for a little flirtation on the side.

Inside the Great Hall where Julius was to play, it wasn't all music. The place was packed, a thousand students, maybe, eating sandwiches and peanuts, calling to each other across the hall. Some girls had transistor radios tuned loudly to different stations. The quieter students slept or read newspapers.

When the curtain went up a couple of guys made long speeches from the stage in very posh accents, calling for an end to Influx Control, demanding equal pay for equal work, less petty *apartheid*, the right of free assembly, no more detention without trial, better canteen food, a licensed bar on the campus, credit cards, less kwashiorkor, more contraceptives, academic freedom and mixed residences. All the speakers quoted Abraham Lincoln: "For evil to succeed, it is enough that good men remain silent." The crowd did not remain silent. They cheered, shouted "Pissorf!" or turned up their transistors. They threw pennies on to the stage, or sandwiches — depending. There was this band of black cleaners in overalls who scouted around with wire baskets picking up all the junk. And there was plenty of it. Let me tell you that you could've put the hungry five thousand of loaves and fishes fame on full board by using just what those guys threw away of their lunch. Then the engineers lit a fire in the aisle. Girls screamed as the flames roared. A dozen guys jumped on the blaze and put it out and were called to the stage to take a bow. The audience cheered and whistled. All this time, through the confusion, noise and smoke a man in a green jersey with holes under the arms was pottering around popping off with a flash camera. I asked Koosie who he was.

"Oh, that's Donald, man. Cat from the Security Police. He takes everybody's pic sooner or later. For the files, dig? Look, I'll show you what I mean . . ." He cupped his hands around his mouth.

"Hey Donnie! Over here." He waved.

Donald scampered over grinning. I tried to cover my face but I wasn't quick enough. Fshht! The lightning struck twice.

First Donally, then Donald. I found myself shivering.

"I'm glad he took my good side," Koosie said.

"If he got you, Koosie, then he'll have me, too."

"Welcome to the club," Koosie said.

At last Julius appeared, thin, built like a walking stick, a permanent curve to his neck, hooked himself over the keyboard and played. Difficult to hear because of the noise which didn't let up, interspersed with shouts of "Yeah, go man!" and "Sweet, old Julius" and "Hit them keys, big J!" After watching Koosie lick his fingers and whistle loudly at the end of a number, I soon got the idea. I told myself it felt good to be part of a multi-racial event but I worried about my photograph.

Koosie hated Raboobie. He told me I should get out.

I told him about Raboobie closing down.

"I know Raboobie. He takes the cash out of the Black man's pocket for his fart-arse zoot suits that didn't cost half he charges. He sucks people dry."

"He's a good guy. He took me in and gave me a job when I was down and out."

"And now he's moving out so he kicks you in the middle of next week. Maybe to you he's a good guy. To me, he's a blood-sucking flea."

"But you buy from him. Your friends buy from him."

He shrugged. "Dogs have their fleas."

"It's not his fault that they're rezoning Melkbos Street for the Railways. He has to go."

"White man's magic, Harry. It moves mountains. Listen, I gotta idea. D'you drive, man?"

He listened impatiently while I explained about having no car. Even if I learnt to drive, I couldn't get a licence without papers and I wasn't registered.

"Who said anything about a licence?" Reaching up he tapped my temple. "I swear your brain's turning into pumpkin pips. You get that way working with Koelies. On the job I'm thinking of you'll be driving a commercial salesman, a cat called Epstein the Traveller. Right there behind the wheel you'll be, in a uniform, the lot. What better licence can you have, unless it's a job driving a dominee? News round town is that Epstein's just lost his driver. Bad accident. And he's got trouble finding a new man with the right skin. He likes 'em not too dark, see. Sort of coffee-coloured. Less trouble getting 'em fixed up at country hotels that way. He'll go for you. Leave it to old Koos. He'll fix you up."

For the next month he came every evening to Melkbos Street behind the wheel of a Buick, a Chev and at least a dozen other assorted limousines and we'd go cruising.

"Which car is yours, Koos?"

"None of this crap. I'm waiting till the right one comes along. For the meantime, I borrow from my friends. I gotta lot of friends."

Raboobie would watch us from an upstairs window. He said nothing but I knew he didn't like it. Then when I told him I'd got a job with Epstein the Traveller he was too impressed to ask questions.

"You moving up in the world, Harry. I'm happy for you. Watch out for this Koosie, that's all. Take the job with my blessing. We're all finished down here."

"Come on. It's not the end. You've got that nice new bit of frontage up town near Blood Lane. You'll be on your feet again in no time."

"Of course I'll be on my feet. But that's because if you lie down they drive over you. You told me that — remember, Harry?"

"But you've got a new place," I persisted stupidly. "It's not the end."

He waved a hand blindly. "Harry, I'm getting out of Maharaj Mansions after twenty years. How do you think I got what you call my nice little place? I'm in hock to the Goolam's cousin, that's how. My whole life is here in this street. Now the bastards are clearing me out. What is this if it isn't the end?"

10

Into my cell come these two guys I know all too well now: Lubavitch and Stokkies. Lubavitch is thin and sandy-haired with a fuzzy down of old Wyner's type covering the many freckles on his face. Stokkies is immensely powerful with cropped hair. He used to be a stoker on the railways, he tells me. He tells me often but sometimes I can't hear him on account of my ears being blocked by something I don't understand but it hurts there, and sings sometimes too, a sound like the radio would make very late on a Sunday night when my father fell asleep in front of it after the Epilogue when the preacher's voice faded away and darkness settled like the cloth on the parrot's cage. They sit in my cell and talk, Lubavitch and Stokkies. They talk for hours, those two. In fact only one thing stops them talking and that is when Stokkies gets up out of his chair and hits me. He could reach me without getting out of his chair since we sit practically nose to nose. But he wouldn't do that. He might not hit me in just the way or in just the place he intends, if he merely stretched. So he stands. A precise sort of fellow, Stokkies. Lubavitch is quite the opposite. He's all heart, old Lubavitch. I know this because he tells me. He tells me when Stokkies goes out of the room for a cigarette. At least, that's where Lubavitch says he's going. Lubavitch says he ought to report Stokkies who is nothing but a thick savage, because he might kill me one of these days. Only, he's a bit afraid to report Stokkies in case he turns around and kills him too. He's quite capable of it, he says. People who don't co-operate drive him mad; and Lubavitch stares at me with his milky blue eyes.

This really should come much later, but sometimes I feel scared that there won't be anything later, so I'm putting it in now. I know they sneak in here when I'm asleep and read what I've been writing. If I stop writing then I get a visit from Lubavitch and Stokkies. My only hope is to keep writing. While I write I'm safe. But I must never stop. While it goes on I will *never* stop.

Epstein the Traveller was small and dark, with a powdery white face as pocked as a Highveld noon. He had more gestures than a busy bookie and was always full of talk. So fond was he of what he called "ideas in action" (he had the ideas, I provided the action), that four weeks with him damn nearly killed me.

"Thing to remember about me, Harry my old sweetheart, is that I'm a going concern — which is a big jump from the nothing I started as, considering I turn over nearly five thou per. Not bad going for a guy who plugged a second year dentistry, bumping down the University steps on the bones of his arse after his old man told him, Lionel, there's no more money — you can call me Lionel, I don't stand on ceremony with my staff, such as it is. It's better business standing on my customers who lap it up — anyway, as I was saying, 'Lionel, go to hell!' barks the old man, and I shoot back, 'O.K. if that's the way you want it, get stuffed, then!' — excuse my French, Harry, and off I go and get a job with old Jeff Topolowski, who wouldn't give you ice in winter, shoves me behind the roped-off Bantu counter where I flog purgatives, skin-bleaches and quack patent medicines like there's no tomorrow, while he struggles to sell his white customers sanitary towels and Japanese hangover remedies, all terribly posh, you see. It taught me a great big lesson, viz: if you go round with your nose in the air, a la Topolowski, it follows that you're going to spend your life staring at the ceiling. Me, I saw the blacks might not buy a wide range of things, but what they bought, they bought big. It stands to reason. You offer a washing girl the chance of turning into a fancy white madam overnight and she's going to beat a path to your door. You could say I saw the light. I left Topolowski to the old vaginal and tired liver business and got myself a dealership from Gloria Sunshine Skin Care Products and went on the road in a beat-up Morris Minor with a roof rack piled to the clouds with 7-Day Wonda Skin Bleach, my trial run, so to speak. It was a sell-out. Later came wigs, toothpaste, washing powder. Everything I sell adds up to one thing Harry, and that's a damn big bucket of whitewash. In a way I think of myself as being a bit like Saint Paul. More than a businessman, a *missionary*, that's me. Except that I'm not out for souls. I'm in the business of saving skins."

Gloria Sunshine was the trade-mark (which is a damn silly way of describing the girl) of Southern Sunday Skin Care Products (Pty) Ltd. These famous preparations were derived, as everybody knows, by one Sampie de Doorns in Krugersdorp, from a recipe discovered by his great-grandmother, Klara de Doorns, who had used it with miraculous results against the kaffir 'flu during the Great Trek. In the beginning he was working out of one room, his garage (or was it the outside lavatory?) In the end, a Stock Exchange restaurant had been named for him and a section of the national highway. Sampie's venture was folk history — hardly surprising in a country where businessmen commonly dreamt of untold riches from some similar coup: a perpetual motion machine; a salted gold mine; a fully automatic gibbet, a car that ran on water. Every week the papers were full of these hopeful cases in which churchmen and politicians traditionally invested and lost enormous sums. Old Sampie's business was to spread so widely that by the time he eventually sold out to Oliver Horak & Associates, the investment trust people, (their Honest Injun Third Party Co. went bust soon afterwards and so many directors fled to Israel it was like a second exodus from Egypt — only this time it was the Indian Ocean they crossed and mostly they went by Comet), old Sampie had scored so richly on the deal that he bought himself a hill in Knysna and named it Mount Gloria. Which is damn appropriate considering that's what most of the country had wanted to do to her for years. The point is that Gloria, or at least Gloria's face and figure, had become part of the great South African family, a sort of national pet.

Gloria's name flogged by the ton suntan lotions, potions and pills, anti-sunburn treatments, dark glasses, infra-red lamps, golfing and beach umbrellas, sun hats and green eye shields. She was an amazing institution. After van Riebeeck's no face was better known. Her picture smiled from the counters of chemists and grocers, billboards and the rear windows of motor cars. Butter blonde hair framing an oval face, propped on an elbow she stretched out naked on a beach as yellow and smooth as a banana-skin, under a dark green palm tree, smiling over a bare right shoulder through enormous sunglasses, perfect teeth gleaming like a picket fence faintly, entrancingly wet, as if recently painted and from her lips came floating in a fat, white speak-bubble her promise to us all: *"Fall in love with Sunshine . . . 'cause Sunshine's fallen in love with you!"* She was a gigantic fraud, of course, and people loved her for it. She looked well. Gloria showed all and revealed nothing. Even the cleft between her buttocks was cunningly hidden by a pyramid of bottles of sun-tan lotion. Schoolboys were traditionally grateful to Gloria: the promise of her nakedness was the closest most ever came to a sex education. Certainly, it was the closest I got in damn near sixteen years (the brush with Mary Smithson aside) to a glimpse of what Brother Donally meant when he warned us about "the unclothed female form" and Yannovitch called the *nood*.

When we were in Standard Six Yannovitch suddenly became interested in drawing after seeing a film on Toulouse Lautrec. I think this had mainly to do with the fact that Lautrec, like Yannovitch at the time, was a dwarf and yet impressive proof that small men got girls. One day he came to school with a drawing of a reclining woman. Her breasts were red and tubular with a heavy swing like a pair of polonies. Topping her thighs a triangular patch of fire-swept bushveld, black and stunted, was bisected by what looked like an irrigation canal beginning in the shallow pool in the centre of her belly, and protruding between her legs like the lip of a tunnel blasted through a mountain. So much for Yannovitch on the unclothed female form. He held a one-man exhibition in the bog during small break attracting a large, enthusiastic crowd. His picture was called "The Other Side of Gloria".

It could be said that Epstein and I worked on the other side of Gloria. With our stock piled in the dusty back window of our blue Opel Car-a-van, we toured the poorer outlets and little dealers Epstein called his rats and mice, scattered thirty miles around: cheap grocers, fake chemists, native trading stores, Greek cafes, witch doctors, holes in the wall, railway stalls, making plenty of stops in the country for open-air demonstrations. We sold Jacaranda Blossom Perfume, White Wonda Washing Powder, Smart Madam Wigs ("Each Hair Guaranteed 100 per cent Human & Fully European"), American Dream Skin Lightening Cream, Ova-Night Hair Straightener and a toothpaste called Zebra in a striped box, ("Brightens Teeth Way Past Belief"). Epstein fitted me out in a khaki uniform with green epaulettes and a peaked cap. He sat beside me in white shorts and bush-shirt with bone buttons, long white socks and buckskin shoes, a talking, walking advertisement for his products. Delighted to have me, he said he was. His lucky day, in fact, because his previous driver had been hit on the head in the Location the day before I applied for the job.

"That's a beautiful skin you've got, Harry. Just the job. I have no end of trouble these days finding the right driver, light-skinned enough to pass for white. When I first started I made the mistake of employing blacks. That was a hairy time. Got 'em to help on the long runs. In this game you're doing hundreds of miles a week in the back of beyond. Reckoned it'd free me to concentrate on the selling side. Well, it went O.K. — to start with. That is, until I tried to put up in the little country hotels in the Platteland overnight. Then I found there were no rooms for the driver. No provision for non-Europeans, see? No food. No running water. No shit-houses. The poor bozies had to kip in the back of the car, parked out in front of the hotel. Well, all it took was for one nosey-parker to see this coon dossing down among the merchandise and he threw a cadenza. You know what these village cops are. Show 'em a strange face and they arrest it. I'd stagger downstairs next morning with a bit of bread or cheese or whatever I could scrounge for my driver only to find — What? Nothing! Not a bloody sausage. Car, driver, goods ... Pouf! And when I wander down to the police station to report the loss what do I discover? You guessed it. Driver in the clink for loitering or not having a pass or winking at the dominee's daughter, car impounded, all my samples held as evidence. Now those were the days when old Oom Sampie was still screwing his hundred thousand a year outa Gloria Sunshine and he, being a good Nationalist rock-spider, didn't like to think he was getting a reputation as a guy who gave strange natives a free snooze in his cars. So he hit the idea on the head. I believe they had similar problems in the European Skin-Care division. A few years ago, after Oom Sampie sold out to Ollie Horak and his tribe, some bright spark gets this idea that, all right, maybe you can't have Africans driving, but, on the other hand, wouldn't it be nice if the in-towns reps have some help. Right, each guy gets a kaffir to carry the really heavy stuff in and out of the chemist shops. Works for a while. Then we start getting these reports. Seems a lotta women are totally pissed-off. Tanning's an intimate thing, see? I mean, the dolly in the question actually sticks her hand into the cream, doesn't she? And then rubs it all over her fair bod. The sight of sweating coons lugging crates of the stuff all pressed to hair chest and sweating groin into the chemists had potential customers retching on the pavements. So the carriers got kicked into touch. Now you know why I'm happy to take you on, Harry. You're light enough to pass for white in the country hotels and yet dark enough to impress my customers who'd give their livers to look like you. You got the skin they'd be proud to be seen in, Harry. You look like a successful kaffir. One the bleach really worked for! You're the answer to a washing girl's prayer!''

It's a pretty ungrateful guy who, having something of great beauty pointed out to him, complains about the dirt under the guide's fingernails. In my first months with Gloria Sunshine under Epstein's direction I began to see something which, each day, looked better to me in every way: namely myself. Of course, nobody's perfect, and I wouldn't say I'd ironed out all my creases overnight. Only a steam-roller would've managed that. My arches still hugged the ground. But during my rounds of the chemist shops I got to know about Dr Scholl's arch supports. I bought a fancy pair in stainless steel and wore them religiously. I found that they eased the pressure on my collapsed arches though I got shooting pains in my calves. My breasts continued prominent but as my chest filled out they kind of spread out around the place rather more, and their summits flattened to give them the look of two fleshy pads, the ends of a life-jacket, say — although uninflated, thank God! Also, my chest hair, now black and spreading, concealed some of the damage, especially on the lower slopes of my twin peaks. I really believed, yes *really*, that I was on my way up. I thought of the dark forces sometimes but was always ashamed of myself afterwards for ingratitude. I looked up to Gloria and she watched over me from every second window in town, on hoardings twenty foot high, kept tabs on my going out even as my coming in, with that sweet and famous three-foot smile over her right shoulder. Doing her rounds I got so dizzy I no longer knew who I was but I felt safe in my uniform, secure on her island with its gentle, yellow, fruity sun, kind blue sky, humble sand. Raboobie was pleased, saw it as the start of a grand career and offered to carry a line of Sunshine products in the new shop.

Epstein did business in two ways. Sales to small shop-keepers and also what he called his "rural sells" on location. These were roadside stops near remote villages, on farms, or behind the sewage works of little dusty towns, but more often than not slap bang in the middle of about a hundred miles of veld with not a soul in sight. Epstein and I would erect this collapsible table and pile it with whiteners. I'd wind up the gramophone and Epstein would shove on something noisy: drums, saxophones and lots of penny whistles. Then we'd wait — never for long, mind you, because in about five minutes flat the veld would be swarming with people. I'd sit them down in long rows in front of the table while Epstein dished out liquorice pipes to the kids and corncobs and a plug of tobacco to the old men. He'd turn the record over. When the congregation were really hotted up and thinking Christmas had come early, the demonstrations began.

First came the White Wonda washing powder. Two identical shirts, a bucket of water splashed in the baking dust and yours truly set to stomping the shirts into the red mud to a chorus of outraged disbelief that good clothes could be treated in such an insane way. The wash followed. One shirt was treated with hard blue soap which the women usually bought. The other was given a good scrub in White Wonda. After rinsing them together I'd hold up the shirts. Gasps of amazement to see such a snow man alongside such a mottled monster. But the masterstroke was still to come. Choosing a woman from the crowd, a poor woman with a string of kids, Epstein would *give* her the clean shirt. And a free pack of Wonda. Cries of amazement. I've seen women break down when he did that.

Then the toothbrushing. Epstein hauled up some old guy with yellow stumps, stood him beside me and ordered us to bare our gums. While we stood there grinning like skeletons he tapped away at our dentures with a blackboard pointer, by way of comparison. Then out would come the Zebra Toothpaste and he gives us both a root-tingling brush, whipping up the crowds who cheered him on until the foam ran down our chins. On what Epstein called a good day, with half a dozen stops for demonstrations, my mouth became so painful I couldn't close it over my bleeding gums.

"Not to worry, my chief," Epstein reassured me. "If you bleed it means you must be in pain. That's good. That's genuine. The more it hurts the more surely the customer knows it's doing you good."

And now to complexion. Mine in particular. Epstein, missionary to the sons of Canaan, was always original — only guy, except for his friend Ralph Swirsky who owned the Boomplatz Pharmacy, ever to hold up my skin as a shining example of the wonder-working power of American Dream. Held it up by the cheek, I might add, with me still inside, between thumb and forefinger, which kind of pulled my smile out of position and made my eyes water. Even so, I flashed the old molars at the crowd and hoped my gums had stopped bleeding. Epstein, slapping my back, called me a real trouper and the tears ran into my smile. They were impressed. But they saved the really big applause, the whistles and foot-stamping, the cries of "Auk!" and "Behold the magician!" for that moment when Epstein, taking my nape with a steadying hand, dropped onto my head a glossy Smart Madam wig, presenting me to what were by then a wildly cheering audience as the complete European ensemble, the God-made white man and everything they'd ever wanted to be. At that point, with Epstein pretending to beat them back but actually shoving them into a manageable queue, they rushed the card table on which stood Epstein's fruits of Paradise, his wigs, bleaches and perfumes — in short, his one damn big bucket of whitewash.

Ralph Swirsky at the Boomplatz Pharmacy in the Queen Mary Location was that one other who loved me for my skin alone. It was a heady experience I can tell you.

"It's your sort of epidermis the Africans want. The trick is to make them believe it comes out of a can. I don't suppose you could spare a little piece. As a sort of sample, you know, the way they do with curtains. I'd have something to show my customers what to aim for. Just a small flap, Harry, from the wrist, say, or a couple of inches from behind the thigh. You'd never miss it. I'd have it mounted on cardboard like those colour-matching charts in paint shops. If you die, maybe you'd consider leaving your hide to science and the Boomplatz Pharmacy. We'd hang it up in a back room like a mackintosh and get doubtful customers to slip it on for a look at themselves in the real thing. Or maybe rent it out to favoured clients as the skin they just got to be seen in!'"

If my stint as driver to the traveller Epstein taught me that it hurts to succeed in the field of race relations, then from our visit to the little town of Godswater, so famous since the trials, I learnt that to triumph is damn near fatal. Epstein had told me that Godswater was his best pitch, taking more bleach per complexion than any comparable town south of the Limpopo. My first visit to Godswater was also my last. Of course, the whole world's heard of Godswater since I was last there. Who can hear it and not associate it with sex and suicide?

We got in one morning at about ten and drove down the main street to the single chemist, Kruger's Apteek, only to find it locked and barred. The same went for Mackie's Supasave General Dealer, on the other side of the town. Locked up too was the Paddekruis Native Trading Store outside the crumbling tin shacks which made up the African location. "Well, I'm buggered!" Epstein said. We drove back into town and double-checked the chemist.

It's not much of a place, Godswater. A filthy great statue of Willem Postma van der Lingen, a slave-dealer who trekked with Andries Potgieter, stood on a plinth at one end of the town, divining rod in his hands and bible under his arm, facing down the main street towards the bank. Founder of the town, old Willem had discovered the underground stream which once fed the reservoir built near the place where the location stands today. Seems he believed that he'd found the source of the Nile. Just the sort of thing the Voortrekkers were doing every day of the week in those days — as Yannovitch used to say: when they weren't discovering the source of the Nile, it was King Solomon's Mines . . . Epstein was pleased to tell me that the underground stream hadn't proved the hoped-for flood, slowing down in the winter to barely baptismal amounts. "Why, Harry man, I'll bet you I could *pee* more in five minutes! Nowadays water must be trucked in from the town of Hermione, ten miles away. Godswater it might have been, but it wasn't the Nile. Just didn't have the carrying power."

Even though the townsfolk kept the name, built three churches in thanksgiving, rounded up the neighbouring tribes, did them the great honour of appointing them "apprentices", worked them till they dropped, and went in for groundnuts on a grand scale, the town never did take off. I guess they did well enough, considering that at the other end of town they built a bank bigger than all the churches.

Epstein jumped out of the car and stood rattling the wire mesh over the chemist's window in a gloomy way, swearing to himself. "Closed in the middle of Monday morning, tighter than a tick's arse. This isn't a public holiday, is it Harry? Not the Queen's birthday or Dingaan's Day, or something?"

Along the length of the main road the only soul to be seen was a legless cripple, sprawled on the pavement, his stumps sewn up in flour sacks, a brown felt hat in front of him in the dust. Epstein wandered over and dropped sixpence into the hat. "Where's the White baas who makes the *muti* in the shop there?" He pointed up the street to the Kruger's Apteek.

The beggar laughed, pointed a fingernail at the sky. Epstein and I searched the clouds overhead.

"Come on, he's mad." Epstein climbed into the car.

"Baas Kruger has gone to jail. Oh yes! In the tronk! They've gone to the jail, my baas," the cripple called after us.

"Bloody fool. This town hasn't got a jail." Epstein took the wheel himself. "We'll go to the police station."

Never one to hang back, Epstein drove into the yard behind the cop-shop. I wasn't prepared for our reception committee. Along the barbed wire perimeter a line of about thirty Black women sat on the ground nursing their babies in the shade of the bluegums. When they caught sight of us a scrum of women rushed the car, waving and shouting. A constable ran from the station and began pushing them back, flicking elbows and backsides with his truncheon and snarling at the babies.

"This is station property," he shouted at Epstein, "you can't park here."

"Listen, man, what's going on? Where is everybody? Is Godswater having a private public holiday, or something?"

Having driven the women back to the fence the cop set about directing Epstein towards the car with hard little jabs in the belly. Seeing their chance, the demented women streamed towards us again, shaking their babies, crying and beating their breasts. "Take no notice of them," the constable says, "they think that you're with the others."

"What others?" Epstein looked around him furiously.

"The butcher, the baker, the candlestick maker. Everyone from the mayor to the police chief, the whole bloody town, they're in it up to here." He lifted a flat hand to the bridge of his nose. "This is not my area, you understand. I'm from Hermione myself. But I was seconded, see, for special duty, while all the others appear in court."

Epstein stuck out his elbows like wings across the door jamb and wouldn't get in the car, but the policeman was a big guy. Epstein's arms buckled and he was shoved in beside me.

"But I've driven damn near a hundred miles, man! What's all this about court? I gotta see my customers."

The angry women reached us, resting their cheeks against the mudguards, clawing at the duco, lifting their babies above their heads as you see crowds on films doing along the routes of coronations and royal weddings. Except we didn't feel exactly regal and instead of cheering and bawling "Long Live the King," they were shouting: "Master, master," and "Give us bread!" and sometimes something that sounded like "Daddy, daddy!"

"Get out of here if you know what's good for you. Stick around Godswater today and all you'll see is your arse, I promise you. These women will bring charges against you, true's God they will. They're lumbering every white man who can rub two balls together." And the constable began his Herod thing again, flailing at the hysterical women and children with his truncheon, growling and showing his teeth.

Epstein's eyes were popping. He started the car and we backed away. In the road he stuck his head through the window. The constable was locking big chains around the gates. "Are you saying that my customers — all of them, mind you, even that tossed-out old Grandpa Stokkies Steenkamp from the Paddekruis Trading Store, who couldn't get it up even if he had three garden boys to help him lift it — that they've been *sleeping* with these women?"

Through the open window the cop hit Epstein one last time for luck on the funny bone. "They weren't playing marbles," he said.

The Godswater trial took longer than expected, owing to a delay in the first weeks when a fancy Lebanese lawyer from Jo'burg, imported to defend the chief of police, produced evidence to prove that the presiding magistrate was himself in it up to his neck and fresh hearings were ordered. There was a further delay when the baker hanged himself. His customers found him the next morning swinging "directly above the doughnuts and a little to the left of the kitke loaves . . ." to quote the newspaper report. Then the inquest on the baker set things back even further. The Sunday papers were packed with pictures of pregnant women, nursing mothers, the baker's family, three tow-headed boys and their mother sitting on a sofa, big dark eyes in chalky faces, under the headlines "No Daily Bread For Them!" The new magistrate was shown in a great centre-page spread, carrying out an inspection *in situ*, checking on whether it was possible to see what the police witnesses said they saw. He lay on his belly in the concrete driveway of the dominee's house, pressing an eye to the crack in the garage doors, smiling bravely and giving the thumbs up. "His Worship Takes It All Lying Down", the caption below the picture read.

I imagined that Epstein would be delighted by his great success in Godswater, because, the way I saw it, that's what it had been. A great testimony to his products. But far from rejoicing Epstein grew pale and listless, bit his lip and for once seemed to have nothing to say. I had to worm it out of him. Eventually he blurted it out. He had had a visit from the police and it had left him badly shaken.

"They blame me, Harry. They say I was one of the cardinal factors."

"They can't mean it. You didn't arrange any of this. You didn't suggest these people break the Immorality Act. Besides, it's a national sport here, isn't it? Love across the colour bar. Like rugby or finger-wrestling. Everyone does it. Housewives with their garden boys, dominees and their nannies . . ."

He threw up his hands and looked anguished. "I told them that. I didn't arrange an orgy. I sell skin products. I'm a salesman not a Svengali. And anyway, I says, people are always doing it. That's why they passed the Act in the first place."

"And what did the cops say?"

"There's this guy. I tell you I didn't like him. Every time I asked what all this had to do with me, he says: 'That's for us to decide, Mr Epstein. Just answer the question.' Where was I — oh yes — I was just saying that everyone does it when this cop chips in — 'Everybody does it, yes. But they don't usually hold rallies and all do it together and that's what happened in Godswater. The whole damn town from the mayor down, have all been dipping their wicks in the black honeypots . . .' " Epstein shook his head and looked as if he was going to start crying. "So I says to the cop, O.K. they're all involved. So why blame me? What's the connection? And this guy looks at me and he says — 'You're the connection, that's why.' Well, I just looked at him. I say — 'Just answer me this: how am I connected?' 'Oh we'll find out,' he says, 'and then we'll have your testicles for bookmarks.' " Epstein beat his hands on the wheel and I had to fight to stay on the road. "And then, Harry, you know what? They took away my passport. Me! Who's never even been to Cape Town! They're mad, Harry. Mad. You can't suspect me, I say. 'I take a wide view, Mr Epstein,' he says, 'I suspect everyone.' "

It all came back to me, then. The man, the cop who had replaced Niewenhuizen who'd thought everyone in Koelietown was a whore. The man who believed in connections. Dekker. And if things ran to form it would be Epstein now, and me next. I knew then I wasn't to be much longer with the traveller Epstein.

I didn't exactly write a letter of resignation to Epstein but I thought I ought to drop him a line, just to keep things kosher. To strike the right tone, I borrowed from the sort of style Charity had developed in the postcards she sent my mother from places like Rustenburg and Machadodorp to which she rushed on the average of once a month to nurse dying relatives. She left, always on Friday, swearing she'd be back by Sunday night. On Monday the post would arrive with the first of the terrible cryptic messages: "My cousin his head she is too sore. We are bad here, but my uncle is worse." Or, "God is willing but my sister's nephew she is dead . . ." To read her you'd never have guessed how good her English was. "I am going Tuesday maybe to be coming or going . . ." her notes always ended. But it was my mother she had coming and going. *"Never* explain", was Charity's motto, "confuse and terrify".

I wrote then: "Dear Baas Epstein — My uncle she is very sick by Port Elizabeth side. I go quick to be with. My heart is sore for leaving such a makhulu baas as baas Epstein. God is knowing. I come back but maybe? Goodbye." — H. Moto (Driver)

I like to think that he was quite touched when he received it (unstamped, of course, so he'd have to cough up at the post office), and went off to show it around to his friends over a beer.

"Here, take a dekko at this. From my driver, well, ex-driver. Good coon, actually. Helluvah articulate to talk to but completely illiterate, as you can see. With the best will in the world you can take a kaffir just so far. Ignore the bit about the dying uncle. Usual sort of crap these fellows give you when they find a better job and decide to move on . . ."

Of course, I never expected him to show my card to the police.

11

Koosie understood why I'd left Epstein the Traveller.

"Sharp shooting, old Chief. If those cops had come nosing around and found this boy, funny colour, crazy hair, with no proper papers they'd push their noses up your trouser leg and never stop sniffin'."

"I told him I was going home to Port Elizabeth."

He eyed me shrewdly. "Do you get homesick for P.E., Harry?"

I coughed and looked vague. "Yes. I miss being out Nahoon way."

He examined his nails. "Nahoon's in East London, Harry, not in Port Elizabeth. I know. I got family there. You gonna be heading for the hills now?"

"Raboobie says I can stay on here for a while. It'll be some months before they demolish the building. Thing is, I have to find a job. I thought I'd try another shop — for some running work."

Koosie gloomed. "You had enough working for the Koelies. My flute's coming along very well. I'll be ready to go to the States soon. Look here, I got a new secret route." And he drew me a map on the back of an invoice. "This one goes through Swaziland. It's known in the trade as the 'Swazi Flier'. You can come with me when I go."

I thanked him. "In the meantime how will I eat?"

"Tell you what. I scheme I can get you a fiver a week — no questions. It'll take a few days to set up. I gotta see a man first. This is a collector's job. At a Roadhouse. Fetching in the trays, plates, glasses y'know, when the fat white cats finished eating."

"You mean that there's a job going as a waiter?"

"Where you been all your life Harry? Waiters is for whites only. But a collector, he's the one who runs out to the cars to collect the dirty dishes for washing up. You know where's the Swiss Cottage Roadhouse, pally? A little bird told me they're losing their kaffir who collects the trays. Leave it to Koosie, sweetie-pie. He'll fix you up."

Raboobie wept a little when he took his leave and warned me about Koosie. "You can't say you know him just because he buys here now and then. And he buys zoot stuff — a waistcoat maybe, or patent leathers, always good stuff, always flash — but a crook, all the same."

"He's a nice guy."

Raboobie laughed. "What you talking, Harry? — Nice! He's a tough guy. He's a crook. I know him, I'm telling you. He's headed for Pretoria Central condemned cell one Monday morning." Raboobie wrapped his fingers, all flashing red, around his pudgy throat and made strangling noises, eyes popping. "He's in very big with the location tsotsis — boys with knuckle dusters. You've seen those boys who come to my shop — Daddy Long Legs Kunene, Genius Matuabathe, Winston "Cheeky" Nene, Walter Zulu — they're gangsters, Harry. They specialise in the pushing of bicycle spokes into the spine, snatching the purses of old women, the stabbing of people who won't pay protection money. Koosie will end up among the condemneds, true as God."

"But he's learning the flute in his spare time. When he's good enough he's going to America."

Raboobie gave a horse-laugh and stared at the sky. "Flute! For that sort, it's always the violin. They like the case, you understand. Ask him what he carries in it and — eh! eh! eh!" Raboobie lined up his fists at his waist and fired machine-gun bursts at me.

"But he's getting me a job at the Swiss Cottage Roadhouse. Mr Raboobie please understand. With your moving, I *need* a job."

Raboobie threw up his hands. "I'm against no job Harry. So fine, you work. O.K. But remember, that doesn't mean you got to share his cell, right? — When they come for him one fine Monday morning at cockcrow."

The Swiss Cottage Roadhouse, out there on the Great North Road, about half a mile after the Belgravia Traffic Circle, was the only place in the Southern Hemisphere that stayed open after midnight. I'd never seen it any way other than after dark, lit by neon and looping fairy lights and headlights of massed ranks of parked cars flashing for service, with white jacketed waiters moving like ghosts between the customers. On Saturday nights Yannovitch did his silver paper trick on his old man's car and took us there after a party. In the daylight everything was different.

"Call on a guy by name of Gawie Puffdot," Koosie told me. "This cat's the sort of manager and cook. Seems I was right about his staff problems — he did lose his collector sudden like. The silly kaffir had a bad accident. This put him in shitstreet because it leaves him not only managing but also fetching in the trays himself. His waiters won't collect trays, you dig? They reckon collecting's kaffir work. You go for the job. It'll be a cinch, Harry. Didn't I tell you old Koos would fix you up?"

In the mid-morning sun Swiss Cottage was a tired, flaking place, stuck up there among gray fields of tarmac with maybe six cars, no more, strung out along the far edges of the parking lot. Four false windows under a mock-Alpine chalet roof were boarded up inches behind the dusty panes, and their lace curtains stapled back with two big cardboard bows.

The life of the place revolved around the kitchen with its enormous glassed-in serving counter running around the four sides of the Cottage. On a display board over the serving hatches were painted by hand all the goodies on the menu, every one a SPECIALITY! There were DOUBLE & TREBLE DAGWOODS! Across the hamburger a lettuce leaf stretching slicker than a ground-sheet, blood-red tomatoes, pale onion rings worming in and out of the dressing and the whole thing cupped and topped by bun-halves painted in vigorous swirls of brown and blonde like the texture of beach sand and studded with sesame seeds. HOT DIGGETY DOGS! One Vienna sausage, escaping springily from the roll, a pink rubber cosh with a hard lethal, sideways shine to it, suggesting what? — a rock-solid centre and smashed teeth, perhaps. Or perhaps nothing but air — cunningly pumped up and ready to go bang at the first bite with, along the side, yellow and thick as a cavalry stripe, a smear of mustard. SUPA DUPA MILKSHAKES AND FLOATS! Two straws, one broken-backed and resting on the rim of the glass, its upright partner toothmarked toward the top by nibbles of enjoyment. Inside the glass in shocking pink and horror-movie green, not liquids at all, but deadly, milky gases met and fixed. Condensation along the sides of the glasses in dark droplets clung or fell. On the roof of the Swiss Cottage balanced a little girl made all of neon, a bow in her hair and one hand split like a branch; the other beckoned to the passing traffic. She seemed to be trying to keep her balance. At night she lit up and the branched hand moved, signalling from the roof with a hitch-hiker's wave. In the daylight the glass tubes that made her body, as if she wore her innards outside, were grey, cold and dusty. Painted on the four walls of the Cottage in letters of fading black four-foot high was the warning: DO NOT HOOT! FLICK LIGHTS FOR SERVICE! I watched as two waiters stepped out across the tarmac towards the cars with fast little mincing steps, loaded trays balanced on the flats of their palms and held up level with their shoulders, and headed for the scattered cars.

I knew the boss when I saw him. He wore this dirty chef's hat like a wilting mushroom. Rows of hamburger patties were fizzing on the grill before him and every so often he'd smack them around with the skillet.

"Mr Puffdot?"

"I've been called worse." He didn't turn round.

"Excuse me, sir, I've come about the collector's job."

"Name?"

"Harry Moto."

He hawked up phlegm, spat into a handkerchief and tossed half a dozen split buns onto the grill. "Hareemoto . . . what kinda name's that? You a Jap, or something? No, never mind, don't tell me. I can pay you fifteen bob a shift, seven days a week, hours nine ayem to one ayem, that's after midnight — understand?" He broke a lot of eggs very quickly with one hand onto the grill and followed them with squares of cheese, prodding with his skillet, cursing and sucking his hand when the hot fat spattered. "Well? Speak or forever hold your peace. I haven't got all day." He pulled off his hat and wiped

his face with his forearm. I say *face* — but that's to say his
face and head *together* . . . they went together, you see, and
it wasn't easy to say where one stopped and the other began.
Bald as a coot, he had this long high forehead which, as it
were, continued his face. What he wore on his shoulders
looked, well, not like a face at all but more like a *thumb*,
actually, on which someone had drawn a face.

"Yes." I answered carefully, as if I'd thought about it.
"I'll come."

"Come?" Puffdot mimicked my tones. "Watcha mean —
come? You're here, aren't you? Step inside."

I waited by the spitting grill while he made up the burgers
and set out the orders on the window counter. When he'd
finished he went over to a big steel cupboard in the corner
and unlocked it. Only then did he look at me for the first
time.

"But you're not a kaffir." He sounded disappointed. "I
thought there was something funny about that name of
yours, Hareemoto, Mata Hari . . . Could be a circus act.
Listen man, 'skaffir work, this tray collecting."

"That's what I am, Sir, a kaffir!" Ever eager to please, I
always was.

His eyes bulged. "Well . . . maybe." He thought about it a
moment. "Ag, what the hell — if you say you're a kaffir,
who am I to argue? Don't mind telling you, I can't keep my
tray collectors. Partly it's Joerie and Jacko's fault. That's my
waiters, see? Hard men, both. But fair, mind you. Trouble is
that them and kaffirs — they're like this!" He shoved his two
fists hard at each other across his chest, like butting rams.
"Also, these kaffirs get tired collecting. I mean there comes
the time when they don't want to go on running back and
forwards from the parked cars to the kitchen and all the
washing up to do after. Get too big for their boots do most
kaffirs, given time. Then one day they throw a bit of lip to
my waiters. Fatal. One thing Joerie and Jacko won't stand —
that's a cheeky kaffir. Next thing I know I gotta a kaffir war
on my hands, I gotta fire the bastards, or the police grab
them and find they don't have a pass. Or they run away. Or
like this last kaffir I just had, until a day or so ago, they go
and get knifed. Some guys jumped him in the location — beat
the living shit out of him and carved him up like the Sunday

chicken. 'Strouble with your average kaffir, unreliable. When he's not getting cheeky, or arrested or drunk, he's being stabbed."

The waiters came to the window to pick up their orders. Short little guys both, with well-greased yellow hair waving back over their ears. Joerie had more teeth than Jacko, I think. Or maybe he just opened his mouth wider. Anyway, that's the only difference I noticed. They wore these white bunny jackets, bone buttons with silver rings in the centre, starched three-corner caps fixed somehow on the sides of their heads, pinned to their hair I suspected, black trousers cut very narrow at the ankle and scuffed winkle-picker shoes.

"This here is Mata Hari, the new kaffir, come to do the collecting." Puffdot jerked a thumb.

"Matawho?" Joerie blinked at me. "Is that a Chinese name or something?"

"You don't get kaffirs in China," Jacko objected.

"When I want your bloody opinion, I'll pull the chain," Joerie said amiably.

"I come from Port Elizabeth." I was hoping to smooth things over.

"What did I tell you, man?" Joerie snapped. "He's from P.E. They've got a helluvah lot of Chinese in P.E."

"You don't have to tell me. Any fool knows that." Jacko turned on his heel. "You think I don't know P.E.? I've travelled a bit. Not like you who's never been further than the station bar. Anyway he doesn't look like a kaffir."

"No," said Joerie. "It's the Chinese eyes."

They loaded up their trays with hamburgers, milkshakes and coffee, balanced saucers on the cups to keep in a little of the heat and set off across the tarmac, swaying from the hips with dainty, expert little steps, trays shoulder high on the long walk to the cars.

"My waiters, Joerie and Jacko. Bloody good men," Puffdot stared gloomily after their waggling backsides. "Don't give 'em no bloody cheek. Both come off the railways, you savvy? Dining-car stewards they was. Tough as old boots, the pair. Give them cheek and they'll kick your backside round the other side." He rummaged round inside the steel cupboard. "One white tunic with red around the neck," he yelled, his voice a metallic boom, and threw behind him onto

140

the floor what looked, when it landed, like a flour sack. "One pair boy's shorts with red stripe down the leg. One boy's tackies with laces." He took his head out of the cabinet and swept the pile of clothes across the floor with his foot. "That's your uniform. Lose any of it, and you cough up. Comes off your wages, see? Wash the stuff yourself. Keep your shoes clean. You're not at home in the kraal now. Use the Gents lavatory to clean in. Also to pee in. I haven't got no non-European boghouse. But if you value your health, don't use it when Joerie or Jacko are in the vicinity. And remember — use of a white lavatory by a non-white is strictly against the law. If the cops spot you, I'm up in court." He pointed to the sink in the corner. "You do all the washing up in between tray-collecting. Use plenty of soap. Keep that corner clean, or the cockroaches build up. You seen cockroaches?" he asked suspiciously.

"Yes, I think so."

"Think so! My, don't we talk fancy? You been to a mission school, then? Jesus, that's all I need. A clever kaffir. Listen boy, the cockroaches round here is so big and smart they'll be asking you out if you give 'em half a chance. Right, that's all you need to know. You stand at the window and watch for the customers to flick their lights. That means they've finished eating. At least, flicking their lights is what they're *supposed* to do, I mean, Christ! that's what's written up there in big, black letters for all the world to see. But you always get the clever bastard who sits on his hooter. When that happens leave him till last. Teaches 'em a lesson. When the headlights go, nip along and fetch in the tray. Don't drop nothing. Breakages is docked off your wages. You get one free meal a day, whenever we aren't busy and after the waiters Joerie and Jacko have eaten. Take your chow out there behind the Gents. Standard menu — hamburger and chips, or hotdog and coffee. Don't let me catch you sneaking any left-overs off the plates you collect. I'm not running a Salvation Army hostel. Right, now nip along and shove on your uniform." He swept up the pile of clothes and threw them at me. "Change in the Gents, Moto, and keep your head down. Remember, it's illegal to have kaffirs in there even if you're not a kaffir. And one last thing — we get lots of courting couples here. Don't let me catch you peeping all

141

googly-eyes through the windscreen just as he's got her tit in his mouth . . . O.K? Some little dolly who looks up to find your fuzzy head staring might think you're out to rape her."

I gave him what I hoped was a reassuring smile.

"What's so funny? Keep your mind on the job and let's have no thinking filthy things about white women. Now go an' get dressed. Don't hang around here like a lost fart in a thunderstorm."

The lavatory was a black hole, ankle deep in urine. Stepping into it in the dark I heard waves breaking against the further walls. I traced the light switch but it took some scouting around before I found a dry spot to change. I studied the messages on the walls. "YOUNG MAN SEEKS GENUINE PROZZIE NO CHANCERS!" Some guy was advertising his cock and he matched his measurements against King Farouk's and Charlie Chaplin's to show how he won by a long head. Several urgent meetings had been set up for 9.20 on 31 May 1952. They didn't say what was on the agenda.

Outside, and changed, I felt the breeze flapping around my knees. With my clothes heavy on my arm, I waited uncertainly outside the Gents. Puffdot opened the window of the serving hatch and waved at me. He stuck his head out of the window.

"Hey, Moto," he yelled. "You stupid bastard! Can't you see that guy down there flicking his lights? Wake up man!"

Holding my clothes in my arms and running uneasily on the sides of my feet because my sandshoes were too small and pinched my toes, I galloped down to the end of the parking area where a man in an old blue Vauxhall with "Kiss Me Sugarlips!" sprayed across the bonnet was flicking his lights hopelessly in the fierce sunlight.

Joerie and Jacko leaned against the serving hatch and watched me, laughing.

"It is not that Joerie and Jacko have anything against you personally," Puffdot told me when he got to know me better, "it's just that they don't like kaffirs on principle. Even if you're not a kaffir . . ."

In my time as a tray-collector at the Swiss Cottage Roadhouse my chest continued to sprout hair at a satisfying rate. My skin turned a good rich teak colour under the sun. I took to leaving the top buttons of my tunic open as I loped from car to car puffing away to myself. I wouldn't have said that my beastly mounds were any smaller but my spreading chest had begun to put a decent distance between them. My flat feet were a different story. The sandshoes Puffdot issued were too small to make room for both my feet and my arch supports. Something had to give. My toes began to take on the stunted compression of Japanese dwarf trees. I cut space for them. This made things easier on my toes but ruined the shoes, loosened them so much that when I ran they would slap on the tarmac of the parking lot with an echo like lonely applause. I'd have said you could have heard me coming for miles. I'd have said, too, that I'd come close to achieving that invisibility I so admired in the cleaners at St Bonaventure's, and had myself begun to acquire — as Gino Ferranti's inability to see me had proved — and which is nature's gift to your common or garden kaffir. Less and less did the customers notice me, and when they did, they more and more took to calling me "John". Oh yes, I began to believe I had really and truly dropped out of sight, that from henceforth the dark forces would no longer bother with me; that I had been tested and found wanting, that I simply wasn't worth destroying.

I bought a bicycle. Midnight and early morning each day I rode the four miles between Swiss Cottage and Maharaj Mansions, with just the creak of my saddle to persuade me that I was going somewhere. At night the answering, echoing smack of the tar under my feet was my only companion as I ran between the kitchen sink and the wrecked trays clipped on the car windows on collapsible aluminium tripods, aswim in coffee, floating crumpled greaseproof wrappers stained with piccalilli and tomato sauce, and my only entertainment the wrestling couples in the front seat, the gear lever between her knees, love-bites along his neck turning green in the neon and the smell of stale air, perfume, sweat, smoke reaching up for me as I unhooked the tray from the window and loped away, my ears ringing with the scratch of nylons, the flight paths of loosening zippers and the electric crackle of someone fighting his way inside someone's stiff petticoats.

So fast did the green paint peel off the walls of Maharaj Mansions after Raboobie left that I began to get the idea that the old place hadn't the heart to hold itself together any longer. One by one the boards went up over the doorways of the shops along Melkbos Street when, as Raboobie had predicted, eviction orders were served and the traders cleared out. Roofs fell in without warning. Windows fogged up and cracked of their own accord with a sound like silk tearing. The street became a favourite animal graveyard. Dogs and cats made the special journey to Melkbos Street in order to die in the doorways. Very soon the only things moving along Melkbos were the paper bills plastering the grimy shopfronts: eviction orders, cinema advertisements, rezoning plans, withdrawal of trading notices, demolition signs and condemned notices, city council planning applications and permissions for the new railway canteen, the railway social clubs, white shops and offices to come. When the wind got up, the street looked oddly cheerful, as if it had put on bunting and was waiting for some strange parade that never came.

My electricity was cut off. I bought a hurricane lamp. The plumbing worked outside in the backyard because the same system supplied water to the marshalling sheds and shunting yards. I washed at the tap near the back fence. Things rapidly gave way. One evening as I climbed the sagging stairs to my room, the bannister from the flight above sailed past me and disappeared through the floorboards into the cellar. The next night a floorboard collapsed under my weight. I took note of this, bought a rope ladder, dropped it down the side of the building and from then on I climbed the outside back wall to my bedroom window each night.

In June it was that the dark forces sent me their card. I'd been with Puffdot about three months and as I set out for work one morning — Jhavari's Savile Row Tailors, a red-brick Victorian front and one of the most solid seeming buildings on the street, collapsed without warning. It killed a railway foreman who happened to be passing at the time. I stopped my bike and stood in the crowd of washerwomen, messengers and railway workers watching the fire brigade digging him out. He was surprisingly unmarked, showing just this bruise about the size of a shilling on his right cheek. His hair and toothbrush moustache were cheese yellow. Well, one side of his face was untouched. The other side, where the building

144

had fallen on him, was pushed in like a cardboard cup grey with masonry dust as if one half of him had aged terribly suddenly. For some crazy reason they fetched his wife. In curlers and carpet slippers she stared at the body and beat her breast. "Oh God," she wailed, "Oh God, why have you done this? He was such a good man, my Kobus." Across the road a bunch of sympathetic washerwomen joined in her grief. "Shame madam, poor madam, sorry madam!" and they lifted their pinafores over their faces.

The waiters Joerie and Jacko spent a lot of time getting pissed off with each other (when they weren't getting pissed off with me, that is). One afternoon, in hot late November it would have been, quiet, without much traffic, the two of them decided to skip off to the Gents, out of sight of old Puffdot, there to polish off a demijohn of sweet Lieberstein. Next thing all hell broke loose. I heard them going at each other hammer and tongs, sloshing away in the urine, screaming blue murder. Puffdot dropped his skillet and ran. But the lavatory sets up this pretty good echo and so I heard old Jacko having his little say. It turned out, according to Jacko's public broadcast (surprise, surprise), that Joerie had begun life as a fully-fledged coloured in a little place called Volstruisgat, a god-forsaken shanty town on the Cape Flats, all corrugated tin and pumpkins on the roof against the raging South Easter; you know the sort of scrubby, dusty howling place they chuck the coloureds into after moving them out on account of all the white folks wanting to build golf driving ranges and art galleries slap bang in the middle of the part of the town the coloureds have been living in from the year dot, ever since Van Riebeeck arrived at the Cape and his crew fell in love with every Hottentot they clapped eyes on. Somehow, in the way these things happen, Joerie had got himself reclassified as a white man and was damn proud of his status and naturally enough we heard him telling Jacko he intended breaking his neck first chance he got. Puffdot went in and dragged them into the sunshine looking like two fighting cocks. Jacko was screaming out Joerie's dreaded secret so loud you'd think he wanted it heard as far afield as Cairo and the commercial travellers were leaning out of the windows of their Fords drinking in the scandal, eyes popping.

Puffdot forced the waiters, biting and scratching every step of the way, into the kitchen, told me to fill the sink, and held their heads under the cold water for as long as it takes to drown kittens. Each time he hauled them up for air Jacko would spit water and start calling Joerie a coloured, a klonkie, a houtkop, a moffie, an Abo, a kaffir and asking him which hottentot had slept with his old lady and in reply Joerie kept trying to knee Jacko in the groin.

Afterwards there was an edgy truce for a time. Then, one day, this couple shows up in an old blue A-Forty. She's pretty with bright red lips and cheeks, and her face slightly shining as if it'd been varnished. Before long the A-Forty's there every night, very late, with just the chick in it, and soon enough she has Jacko hopping in the A-Forty when he comes off duty and thumbing his nose at Joerie who goes home on his enormous antique Harley Davidson on which he lies spread-eagled, on account of his being so short, as if he were riding a buffalo.

Jacko was very full of himself now because he had this girl and was forever stopping alongside the driving mirrors of parked cars after delivering a tray and pulling out an aluminium comb he kept in his sock to pamper his hair for minutes on end until some smart-alec driver told him to go and have it permed. Joerie seemed very impressed because Jacko was catching this cheap thrill with such a hot-looking dolly and quietened down a lot, out of respect, and one day summoned the courage to very humbly ask Jacko her name and Jacko told him that it was Henrietta but warned him that he'd better not get any ideas because she was *his* date and Joerie could bloody well eat his heart out.

Well, when Jacko was so crazy about Henrietta that he didn't know if his name was Angus or Agnes, Joerie gives him the big news. Henrietta, he spelled it out for Jacko, was his cousin. What was more, she didn't carry white identification papers. And that meant old Jacko had been going out with a coloured. So old Jacko had better keep his great big trap, which was bigger than the big hole in Kimberley, tightly shut about who was and who was not a coloured. Otherwise the cops would be knocking at his door in the middle of the night asking why he was kipping with coloured girls and they'd cart him off to the cells, arrested under the Immorality

Act, and his underpants would be exhibit A in the trial and he'd go to jail for about a thousand years. Jacko said very bitterly that Joerie would have used his own mother to get even and Joerie said Jacko was damn right he would too — and Jacko added — if she hadn't run off with a Xhosa debt collector. And there was the last we saw of the A-Forty.

Since they could get no further with each other they firmed up the truce and laid into me. I reminded them of all they didn't want to remember. It's the old story.

"Listen Mata Hari," Joerie said, "I'm kinda confused about your looks. Are you a coloured or a koelie?"

"Who me?" I tried to look surprised.

"Who else?" Joerie said and he cast an eye around the place, then up in the sky and down on the ground. "I don't see anybody else I could be talking to. Do you, Jacko?"

"Now that you come to mention it, no I don't see no one else, Joerie. Unless you count this kaffir boy here."

Joerie stared at me. "He's not black enough to be a kaffir."

"'Snothing," Jacko said, "he's a white kaffir."

And they both fell about laughing, holding their sides. Then they picked up their trays shoulder high and set out for the cars, bums waggling like pert mannequins.

I dream a lot, possibly because I'm lonely. It's not a crime, dreaming. But it's a mistake. Afterwards, I feel more lonely than ever. Never go out on a limb, I decided, unless you're planning to swing from it. I dream of a slackened bow, lovely curves rising to points where the nipple, like a firm, pink knot stands out, and there is nothing between the lines but air, only I don't know that in advance. I'm dreaming of Mary Smithson's breast. I go to cup it firmly. But to expect firmness, I remind myself in my dream, is the same mistake I made once buying candy floss at the Easter Agricultural Show. Its smooth white tissue wrappings gave the look of something solid beneath, then fell away to nothing, astonishing the hand. Thus Mary's left breast, faint moonlight on it, once. I wake up feeling hungry after dreams like that. I have no right to feel hungry. I am fed regularly — "to keep up my strength," they say. This irritates me. In the first place I do not feel especially strong. And, secondly, for what reason should my strength be so kept up? Except to continue writing this down — something they wish finished but which I'll keep up as long as they continue to require it. They marvel at the way I go on. Writing, they say, is sheer kaffir work.

There's something dreadful about coming across a corpse in the early morning, especially on one of those rare, grey days that looks like turning to rain. Something about sunshine encourages the game of life. It can even help the dead for a short while to look just a shade less dead. Come to think of it, the sun shines pretty well continually out here and that probably helps to disguise the fact that half the damn country's deceased.

When the front wall of Jhavari's Savile Row Tailors fell on the railway foreman and I watched them dig him out, the sun shone on his dusty yellow hair and being unmarked, seen in that light, he looked alive but asleep. Left to itself, on a dull morning that looked like turning to rain, the skin seems more quickly to set grey and hard in the way tar does drying on the road. On a morning of low, spitting skies, after the *tsotsis* got her, that was how Mama looked. She was stiff, cold and grey and quite impossibly contorted. I'm speaking of those parts of her I could see. She was the first thing I saw as I reached the bottom of Melkbos Street where the statue was. Thing is, she was wedged in between two steel stairs, face down, hanging directly over what was left of her fruit stall. They'd jammed her in really hard like they were trying to slice her in three. I don't know whether she was still alive when they did that. Quite certainly she was dead when I came past. Bits of splintered boxwood were scattered everywhere; soft messes of peaches and plums had been well trampled by then, and squares of white and blue tissue paper — their wrappings — blew about the stairs. Apples, round and hard, easily rolling, escaped crushing and lay in the dust, many of them bruised where they'd been kicked aside by the passing crowds. The crowds did not stop. Nothing at all, not Mama, not death, not the police about to cover her with a blanket, could hold back those crowds the trains brought in, the swirling, early morning commuter rush from the townships and locations; the Queen Mary, Blackpool City,

148

Elizabethville, the kaffirs come to do the kaffir work and they squeezed past, or hopped over Mama as if clearing a puddle. Mama was bleeding from somewhere, a steady drip like a leaking tap, spattering the apples, making the brown dust pucker and float in tiny red pools beneath the stairs. The air choked with the smell of broken fruit. Old Mama hanging up there reminded me of something. I couldn't think of what it was.

A policeman walked up to me, tapping his cap-peak with his truncheon, an angry little drumbeat, the sound we got with a playing card pegged into the wheel spokes of our bikes. "There's nothing for you here," he said. "It makes me sick what these kaffirs do to their own people. Now bugger off before I run you in."

Mama had laughed when she'd seen me on my bike heading out to the Roadhouse. "Oh yes, yes! Go fast, go fast, Runner-Like-The-Wind, on your big *fiets*. But the white man or the *tokoloshe* or the *tsotsis* will still catch you!" And she jigged about on one foot in an agony of merriment.

The white man, the *tokoloshe* and the *tsotsis*: Mama had known a thing or two about the dark forces. I looked back at her sprawled and dripping on the stairs with the policeman walking up and down impatiently tapping his cap-peak with his truncheon at the crowds pouring down the iron stairs. The feeling was so strong, a picture or something — she reminded me of something but I couldn't think what it was and that made me more sad than anything else.

One Friday night, about a month ago, or a week after Mama was murdered, depending on how you set your calendar, I loped down in the usual way to collect this tray from a Triumph Herald. I grabbed the tray and was just folding away the three legs with a snap preparatory to toddling back to the kitchen when I stopped. I didn't mean to stop but in the back of the car I saw this girl, her head up against the seat, thighs wider than a wishbone and twice as white with the light on them, this babe right, and between her legs this guy, pants to his knees, was bearing down on her from the top of the front seat. For God's sake how athletic can you get? His bare arse was waving around near the roof light like a pair of half-moons. It was an incredible sight and I guess I sort of,

149

well, *peered*. I mean I was so taken up with the whole thing that it took me a moment to realise what it was I was seeing and even longer to realise I had been seen. It was the crouch that did it. By crouching for a better view I drew just about level with the girl's head which was resting against the window. She goggled straight at me, wide-eyed. Next thing I saw her shaking her head violently and thought for a moment she was trying to warn me off. In fact, as it happened, she was trying to shake off her boyfriend's kiss. I know that because when she managed it, she started bawling her head off. I tried to turn the crouch into my best "Excuse me, madam, but I'm just the native boy" cringe, together with a little wave and smile to show her I wasn't dangerous and hadn't really noticed anything. Then I took the tray and started back. Behind me she was baying at the moon. I heard the door of the Triumph open behind me and next thing this bare-bottom chap, still buttoning up, took a running kick at me. His kick missed me but collected the tray and all around I heard plates and glasses smashing. Joerie and Jacko wandered over and drank it in. A crowd gathered. He had better luck with the second boot, connecting with my gut and for some time I couldn't see or speak. He hauled me to my feet and hit me in the mouth. I spat blood down my tunic.

"Those breakages will set you back a couple of quid, Mata Hari," Jacko says.

"This bastard was peeping at my girl and me," says the athletic lover, a bit thrown by the damage he had caused.

"I saw him," announces the nearby driver of an Oldsmobile, "cool as you please, staring in through the window of the car. Hullo, mate, I says to myself, that effing nog's seeing what he didn't oughter. Cheeky swine! We can't have that. Another second and I'd have lumbered him myself."

"All these kaffirs are the same," Joerie says, "no fuckin' respect."

The crowds grew fast. People came over to stretch their legs, and stood around hemming me in. I lay where I fell, holding the tray, surrounded by smashed crockery. I had this vague idea that if they attacked me I could use the tray as a shield maybe.

When Puffdot marched out of the kitchen the crowd fell back. I could see his chef's hat approaching over their heads.

The finger puppet head bent over me. "What's with you, Harry?"

I opened my mouth but nothing came out.

"He's a bloody Peeping Tom," the bare-arsed wonder yelled. "I got him just as he started to run away."

"He's smashed every bloody thing on the tray, Mr Puffdot," said Jacko. "Quid's to thirty bob's worth, I'd say."

"What were you doing at the car?" Puffdot stared down at me.

The crowd was thick around me. I stared 'em straight in the knee-caps. I tried not to laugh but it sounded funny asking me that. "I wasn't doing anything except my job. I was collecting the tray."

"Don't be cheeky," Puffdot said.

"If there's one thing worse than a kaffir," Jacko told everyone, "it's a cheeky kaffir."

The crowd made a happy cooing sound at that, a noise I took to signify their full agreement. They sounded like a bunch of trainee guards in a concentration camp who've just heard how the shower system works.

In the morning I was waiting when Puffdot arrived to open up. He was a bit calmer and let me change my blood-stained tunic for another and didn't charge me. I appreciated that. Then he gave me a week's notice.

"I told you, Mr Puffdot, I meant no harm last night. I collect the trays, right? That's what you pay me for. But to do my job I got to get up close to the cars."

"The way the dame tells it you got so close your nose dented her nipple."

"That's a bit of an exaggeration, actually."

He stared into the traffic. "I know that. You know that. O.K? But I got to think of my customers. The way they see it, you saw too much. That's the thing about being a tray-collector, see Harry? You gotta know what not to see. It's a delicate business. I mean the waiters, they got no problem because they come in at the start of the courtin'. It's afterwards when they've polished off their toasted cheese and downed a milkshake or two, that the guy will make his play. He's just easing her panties down around her knees or maybe she's teasing his dick outa his scants and it's then that you have to appear and disappear — preferably at the same time and with the tray, of course. You have to get that tray or otherwise they'll sit there doodling all night and I'm not running a bladdy motel. So I sympathise with your problem. A tray-collector who knows how to come and go like a shadow is a guy you can trust. There's a lot of trust in this business. I warned you when you started here — it's *delicate*. Hell, I don't want to fire you, Harry. Anyway, where am I going to find another collector? It's kaffir work that even the kaffirs don't like doing. But even though I'm sorry to lose you I reckon I've done you a favour. Tray-collectors who don't know when to disappear is likely to be lynched. Strung up from the little neon lady over there." He jerked his chin at the glass Heidi on the roof of the Cottage, cold, grey and dusty in the middle morning sun. "I'll let you work out your week's notice at double wages. Just to help a bit. And I'm sorry, Harry. Really sorry."

That morning Koosie showed up in a dirty great yellow Pontiac, posing as a second-class taxi, parked it opposite Swiss Cottage on the side of the main road and sat, waving, hooting and *even*, the cheeky bugger, flicking his lights until I'd no option but to go over to him.

"For God's sake, I'm *working*."

Koosie leaned his elbow out of the window showing off his cuff-links, heavy gold, big as baby grands. He squinted over his shoulder. "Don't look now, Harry, but you're in big demand, boy. Here comes the baas. Maybe he gives you a rise?" Koosie flashed his perfect teeth.

Gawie Puffdot had left the kitchen and stood across the road. The traffic flowed between us, shining, molten. His chef's hat stuck up above the roofs of the cars like a crooked chimney. He had his hands cupped around his mouth, the sun on his teeth. I could see his tongue, the sunlight was that bright. "Moto, you lazy good for nothing bastard," he screamed, "get your arse out of there before I kick it into the middle of next week!"

"Friend of yours?" Koosie asked.

Puffdot was so mad he risked the traffic, crossing like a man going into cold surf, both arms up against his chest, elbows level with his armpits, upon his toes and spinning sideways when a three-ton truck or pantechnicon passed too close. Reaching us he rested his belly on the car bonnet a moment while he caught his breath. He ignored Koosie. "You outa your tiny mind?" he demanded. "Last night you're sneaking round like the panga man giving pups to every respectable doll out for a milkshake and a cheap thrill. This morning you're hobnobbing with kaffir taxi-drivers. But then you people got no appreciation, right? You could've been castrated last night. I saved you. Next thing you're bunking off for a chat with your mates. This isn't a bloody beerhall, y'know!"

"Sorry, my baas," Koosie says.

"Speak when you're spoken to," Puffdot snaps.

"Sorry, my baas, but I come to tell this boy here that he must come quickly because the auntie of his cousin is dying in the location."

"And who might you be, my boy?"

"Please baas, but I am this boy's cousin."

Puffdot looked at Koosie and then at me. "You don't look like family."

"Oh yes. We're a big family, baas. Port Elizabeth."

"Oh ja? Then why aren't you at home in Port Elizabeth?"

"We come from there, but we don't stay there. It's a bad place my baas, for us. It makes my heart very sore."

"I don't know about that. There's my sister down in P.E. Nahoon, actually, you know it? She's happy enough."

"Port Elizabeth is a bad place for us," Koosie says carefully, "all of it, except Nahoon, which is a beautiful place. But the baas must know Nahoon is in East London."

"Port Elizabeth, East London, it's all the same to me." Puffdot was fascinated by the car, and peered into the window rubbing the blue vinyl seats, stroking the moulded black leather facia with its glittering gauges, fiddling with the tumble switches. "This is a nice car you got."

Koosie watched this with a shy, anxious, idiot smile as if he were really incredibly grateful that Puffdot wasn't too stuck up to care about his car. "Oh no, my baas, this is my uncle's car. He has sent me with it to bring this boy back with me to our auntie." He leaned across and opened the door. "He must come straightaway."

"But he's on duty! There's trays to collect." Puffdot took off his hat and showed us the thumb on his shoulders where his face had been.

"Not that I want to stand in the way of the dying, mind you. I've got family myself. And I'd like to show that firing Harry was nothing personal. If I say all right, then, Harry can go, you'd better be sure he's not out all day. I'm not running a holiday camp."

Koosie laughed like it was the best joke in the world. "Oh no, my baas. Thank you, my baas. I won't keep this boy away for long. I bring him back as soon as our auntie is dead."

Koosie drove through the rich suburbs that lay to the north of Swiss Cottage, where splendidly large houses are set well back from the road in acres of shaven lawn which lies lush and brilliant in the sunshine under the hissing sprinklers, turning, in the cool places where the shadows gather, to a dark green baize with the smooth nap you see on billiard tables. There is much to admire in a good South African garden, cool, watered, emerald places where by all the laws of nature there should be nothing but baking veld, great dry rustling grass, and dust. Of course, more than the luxuriant plant and bird life, more than the poinsettias, magnolias, flame lilies, roses, the swallows, hoopoes, bokmakieries and wagtails, what flourish above all in a South African garden are the garden boys – nowhere else can they be seen in such a broad and satisfying variety: there are the important craftsmen, treasured professionals in tailored sky-blue tunics splashed with the scarlet monograms of their owners, who dig, manure, fork and mow with expert precision; there are the dignified old greybeards draped in their masters' cast-off white office shirts put out to grass now in some shady corner after a lifetime's service because of their failing eyesight, pressing noses to the lawn and moving slowly on hands and knees in tight circles like tethered goats, pulling weeds; and everywhere there are swirling bands of young apprentices, chirruping schools of piccanins set to work among the hedges or picking up stones, or hunting cutworm, hopping among the flower beds with the sun gleaming blackly on their bare calves, like great crickets. But the scene did nothing for Koosie's depression. He rolled down the window, spat once or twice, and shook his head: "Stupid coons," was all he said.

Then at last he told me.

"Harry, the cops, they put the finger on me. They wheeled

me in to see the number one God, no less! The *makhulu baas*
— and what's worse, they did it just as I'm going to jump this
lovely lady, this *real* babe, Dolores Nkwenzi. I mean, there I
am in the servants' quarters at the back of one of those big
houses on the Ridge, you know the sort of place I mean,
slasto and acres of washlines and a loquat tree, true Africa, a
land where no white man's set his foot, and I'm thinking
myself safe and sound and I got my pants down, Harry, when
the *boere* smash through the door and haul me off to the big
hotel. What timing, what rhythm these fat cats got!" He spat
bitterly out of the window and shot his cuffs. The baby
grands gleamed gold and chunky.

"The big hotel?"

"Sure." He stared at me. "You don't know it? Everybody
knows the big hotel. The cells, man, in the Central Police
Station, Main Street, where Dekker is the number one
bastard. That's where I spent last night. I was one unhappy
kaffir. You know this Dekker? He took over from
Niewenhuizen — who thought everybody wanted to jump the
whores in Koelietown."

"Dekker's the one who frightened Epstein — and lost me
my job. It seems he frightens most people."

"He's fatal," Koosie said. "Everything's politics for Dekker.
He told me — 'I know you my boy, you're an agitator.' Not
me, I told him, I'm a musician. Jazz flute. 'Oh yes,' he says,
'tell me about *apartheid*.' 'I don't know nothing about
apartheid — I don't know nothing except jazz flute. I swear
by my mother and father, sir, I study jazz flute.' 'They say
you plan to slip the country,' he says. Sure, sure, I told him,
I'm going to America one day — to study. 'To study,' he
chaffs me, 'is that what you call it? Which route are you
taking — the Swazi Flier? The Bechuana Jump?' "

Koosie gazed at me, anguished. "How did he know about
my secret routes?" He winced at the memory and threw a
hand up to his face as if to ward off a blow. His small pink
palm fluttered like a leaf.

"Perhaps he was bluffing."

Koosie shook his head. "He drew the maps," he said
hopelessly.

A big grey Chev appeared from nowhere and overtook us,
cutting in and sharply forcing Koosie to slam on the brakes,

155

and then settled in front of us, making us crawl. Koosie swore, dropped back and at the first chance accelerated past the Chev. "Peasants," he yelled, "old women!"

The two men in the Chev watched us go by with grave interest and did not return the two fingers Koosie flashed in passing.

"What did Dekker want you for?"

Koosie shivered. "He wanted to offer me permanent accommodation. My own room, you know — for a long visit."

"I mean, why did he arrest you in the first place?"

At first Koosie did not reply. He lit a Mills and blew smoke into the windscreen. Again I got the impression he was embarrassed by something, afraid to speak out. Eventually he said: "The cops, they came and took Tweetie Boy — him who said he was the big tough man in the township, but all he's got, I'm telling you, is a big mouth that opens like double garage doors — like this — " his jaws gaped " — and he sings like a bokmakierie. He gives them every name he can think of — and for what? They still gonna stretch his neck one fine morning. Anyway, so they got Molefe and after that they got Cheeky Nene and even, get this, *even* Walter Zulu who in fact is clean, clean, clean, like he's been scrubbed every day in Lifebuoy soap, because, but natch, it's never Walter who does the damage but his boys, you dig. But they sent the van for Walter all the same, they wheeled the kwela-kwela right up to the front door of his bladdy big house there in the township ... 'Spring kaffir,' they told him." Koosie licked his lips and rolled his eyes. "Then they came for me. You see, with this Dekker, the whole world's joined up." He laced his fingers together across the steering wheel. "It's like this: Tweetie Boy, Walter, Cheeky Nene and me — we're all involved. Even old Koos who never wanted to do nothing more than play the jazz flute and go to America one day."

"But why? What has Molefe done?"

Koosie made this funny sound in his throat and wouldn't look at me. "There was this old fruit seller, see — Mama we called her. You must have known her, everyone in Koelietown knew Mama. Well, Mama paid a little cash each week to Walter for keeping the *tsotsis* away from her stall. It is an old custom — everyone does it. Mostly Walter's wife Doris collected Mama's kick. You know Doris? Lovely lady, very glam — anyway, at this time it happens Doris was sick so it is, God knows why, that the madman Molefe is sent to collect. Only Mama won't pay. This boy can get stuffed, she says. Only to Doris does she pay, she tells Molefe, and he, Tweetie Boy, can drop dead and she'll have the pleasure of dancing on his grave. Well, that's no way to speak to Molefe, especially not when he is zonked to the eyeballs on *dagga* and *skokiaan*. With Molefe you pay or *vrek*. End of story."

I could see Mama dancing on Tweetie Boy's grave, doing a little jig on her horny, black feet, kicking up her heels so high they bounced off her bottom, just as they did when she used to show me how the white men would come and kick all the Indians out of Koelietown one day. Poor Mama on that bleak grey morning, the last time I'd seen her, jammed upside down in the steel steps of the railway bridge down which the workers poured each dawn and dusk in their thousands as if they were Italians on their way to see the Pope, only they weren't. Mama dripping, like an old, over-ripe, weird, too soft fruit, swollen and torn by the birds, hanging on her iron tree.

"I'd better get back. Puffdot will be after me."

"Sure, man!" He seemed relieved. I knew there was still something he hadn't told me. He leaned across and patted my shoulder. "Bit of a word in your ear, Harry. When in doubt, give a good cringe. Boy, did I cringe last night in the big hotel!"

"Is that why they let you go?"

He stared at me blankly. "You're confusing me."

"Well, it's odd, isn't it? I mean, why go to the trouble of hauling you in only to let you go?"

"Be wise, Harry. This Dekker, he's God in the Central Station. He can do whatever he likes. Why must I complain? He picks me up, he kicks me out. That's how God is. Maybe tomorrow he grabs me again and breaks my head. You never know with God. So in the meantime I'm off — old Koosie's making the jump."

The Swiss Cottage loomed up, dry, dusty, sad in the sunshine. Little Heidi, her painted smiling face fringed with blonde hair, oblivious of the blackened tubes of her body, waved her branched hand: Go back, go back, she seemed to say. I could see Puffdot moving at the grill behind the serving hatch against which Joerie and Jacko lounged, bored, picking their teeth and pulling at their bunny jackets. Business was slack.

"Which way are you going? The Jump? The Flier?"

Again he looked nervous. "Sorry, Harry. Can't say. It's nothing personal, right, but after the heat I got in the big hotel, I can't tell no one about this route. Man, this one's so secret there isn't even a map!"

"It's good of you to come and say goodbye."

"I'm not here to say goodbye. I'm here to tell you to get your arse out of this neck of the woods. I told you — with Dekker everything's joined. Everything, Harry. You got to run."

I understood at last why he had seemed so embarrassed, what it was he couldn't bring himself to tell me. I understood and even as I understood I found myself shaking my head.

Koosie gazed at me horrified. "If you don't — you're dead. Dekker — he wants you!"

"It's not that I don't want to run, Koosie — I can't run. That's to say, I can't run because that's what I do already. That's what I've been doing always." I pointed to Puffdot who'd seen us and was walking across the tarmac with that purposeful stride you get in policemen and doctors who are obliged to make short strolls in public for special reasons. "It's my job — running. I've been running ever since I can remember."

Puffdot leaned on the door and pushed the great thumb with the face on it through the window. "Everything done?"

"Oh yes, my baas, thank you — everyone is dead now. You can have this boy back." Koosie reached across and opened my door, and as he did so he whispered, "Watch this, and watch good." With an apologetic smile at Puffdot he climbed out of the car. He took Puffdot's sleeve and sort of leaned over it as if he was going to use it to wipe his nose or forehead. Puffdot pulled back startled but Koosie held on and suddenly crumpled from shoulders to knee, dissolved, shrank with a wavy motion actually inside his clothes, seemed before my eyes to grow smaller, meeker, bent even closer to Puffdot's sleeve, while with his other hand he scrabbled in his hair tugging at the black curls. "Thank you my baas, with all my heart, I thank the baas for letting this boy come with me to the death of his family member," Koosie said. "The baas is a good baas and will have much happiness in heaven, also many children and much money." As he spoke he leaned lower until he was almost bent double, fastened like a great broken-backed insect on Puffdot's wrist now kissing it. Puffdot stared and tried to break free but Koosie hung on grimly, scratching away at his curls and in between wet sucking kisses he raged on about the great kindness Puffdot had shown me. Then I saw the magic begin to work. Puffdot stopped trying to escape and began to smile and nod, soaking it all up — he even went so far as to give Koosie's shaking shoulders a little tentative pat. Then, as quickly as it had started, it was over. Koosie straightened and disengaged in one movement and was behind the wheel and backing out of the parking lot before anyone had realised it. I knew then what it was I'd been watching: it had been Koosie's goodbye present . . . he had given me a lesson in cringing.

Moments later the grey Chev I'd seen earlier pulled into the parking lot. The two men had hot dogs and milkshakes. They stared at me quite openly when I collected the tray. The driver was tall with red hair and a milky complexion covered with freckles. His partner was short with a head like a lantern. Broad around the temples by an extra band of bone tapering to a square, sheered off jaw. It was, though I did not know it, my first glimpse of Lubavitch and Stokkies. But looking at them looking at me I knew the reason why Dekker had been prepared to let Koosie go. When Dekker had let him sign out of the Big Hotel, Koosie had led him straight as an arrow to me.

IN AGAIN

12

As it happened Dekker didn't reach me first. In the race for which Koosie's visit had been the starting shot, a sort of invitation stakes between the various representatives of the dark forces (first prize, a bursting goatskin of my blood), it was the ghosts of my past who ran out clear winners. It isn't all that surprising, I suppose — though I didn't think so at the time, and have been punished accordingly by being made to think of virtually nothing else ever since.

Great thing about the past is the way it likes to stick around, likes to tag along behind you. You may push it away and deliberately ignore it; you can even forget about it for long stretches. But it never forgets about you. That was the opinion of Stokkies, often repeated. His friend Lubavitch held similar views and though a man of few words he had ways of making his opinion felt. The past was like a dog, they believed. Look behind you and there it was dogging your footsteps. I called them sadists. Stokkies was shocked. Lubavitch denied this. They weren't sadists, he said . . . they were Englishmen. Question was — what was I? The answers lay in my past. It was no fault of mine. It was an accident they would help me make sense of. Just as the breeze was enough to lift Gino Ferranti's protective shirt sleeve to show his withered polio-stricken arm, the skin drawn tight on the stump, slender, like a plastic bicycle pump, so they were there to lift the curtains I had drawn over my past.

I say that if the past is a dog, then it bit me (and it's probably rabid).

Very much later that evening a big, blue Mercedes parked in a far corner of the great tarmac lot where the lights rarely reached near the national road, began flicking its lights for tray collection and I loped down to it in my customary, flat-footed way, knowing, as you know these things after you've been collecting a while, that the customers weren't quite ready. It was as I took up my customary, strategic position beside the driver's window and began rattling the tray in an irritating fashion calculated to speed the tardy client, that the voice spoke, suddenly, peremptorily, from my past: "Just one moment, my boy," it commanded, "the madam is still finishing her coffee."

Instinct saved me. I straightened and stood head and shoulders above the car roof, and nothing could be seen of me but the three top buttons of my tunic; bone buttons with metal circles in the centres. I took a deep breath, knowing it would have to do me for a good while and froze. A small mean wind found my baggy shorts and flapped at them. The stars were high and cold, Cygnus and the Southern Cross and the Milky Way, a dazzling rich fracture in the sky arching overhead, like a shattered windscreen: I devoutly wished I were dead.

There were three, perhaps four others in the car, not counting the driver, because I already knew who he was. I knew even before I'd looked towards the sound of his voice and saw him, instantly recognisable despite his smart houndstooth sportscoat and blue silk cravat which clashed dreadfully with his red curls. It was Theo Shuckel.

Into my head there came ridiculous phrases. I did not want them there, but they came anyway. Things like, "Gosh, Theo, long time no see," and "Good God, who'd have thought it — after all these years!" and "I'm just fine thanks and how's yourself, you old bugger?" Desperate, desperate stuff ... And I think in my state of shock I would have blurted them out had I not been stopped dead by an emphatic crash of cup and saucer, and voice number two, tight, snappy and mean, the audible equivalent of the rubber bathing cap she had pulled, cruelly squeaking over her head to hide her beautiful blonde hair, on those hot afternoons at Jack Wyner's place, many lifetimes before ...

"Ex-*cuse* me! I might be just an ordinary, dull teacher who knows *nothing* about politics but I'm a South African, and one thing I *do* know is that you'll never change a kaffir, sorry, native I mean, until you teach them to help themselves. It's been proved. Besides, things are changing. But you can't alter everything overnight the way these mad students like John Yannovitch want to do, with talk of bombs and revolution. Truly, I never thought John would turn against his own kind the way he's done — but then he never was a *proper* European, only a Pole, or something like that." The madam was Mina.

A third voice chimed in with the predictable bossiness I remembered so well in old Rick van Dam: "Excuse *me*, but he isn't a Pole, he's a Czech, is old Yannovitch. But I agree with you: he's bomb-happy. I think, personally he got into politics because it's more fun than quantity surveying. But it doesn't *mean* anything, the talk, the marches, the demonstrations! These guys aren't going to change anything. Besides, the police watch every move."

From the darkness of the back seat there drifted a fourth voice, soft and round it was, like poured cream, floating out to me on the darkness. "John Yannovitch is a Yugoslav, not a Pole or a Czech, and I think, to be fair, we must call him a revolutionary. That's why he's at University — to learn about revolution, which is one of the three Rs of a good South African education."

It was Mary. As far as I could judge she was sitting right behind Shuckel and so close to me that should she lean to her right an inch or so she would probably see me. I took hold of the roof gutter and pulled, curving over the tray in a desperate attempt to cut her angle of vision. This was incredibly uncomfortable and my calf muscles began to twitch with the strain of it. The breeze found its way under my loose tunic and lifted it like a marquee around my belly.

"Of course, the police watch them. They watch every move," Mina said. "The police aren't fools." I decided she was also in the back, beside Mary. I got the floor plan; evidently van Dam was next to Shuckel; boys in the front, girls in the back.

"Excuse *me*, but the police *are* fools," Shuckel said. "And so are the campus radicals. I think they need each other. It's a sort of game they play together. They go to the same parties, you know. I wouldn't be surprised if they sent each other Christmas presents. The big-deal subversives go out of their way to be kind to the Security Branch. They make their plans at the tops of their voices in canteens and lecture halls, use the phones, though they must know they're tapped, write letters which the cops read practically before the ink's dry. I mean, Jesus! Why don't they take advertising space in the papers? The police repay them by arresting them often and boosting their reputations on campus."

"If revolution is one of the three Rs of a good education, what are the others?" van Dam wanted to know.

The silky voice rustled and spread through the darkness, dreamy, half-amused and strange, as if it came from nowhere and with a kind of weariness in it I did not understand and did not much like. "To give them in proper order, I suppose I should have said, first, 'rugby'." She seemed to be putting a special effort into pronouncing her words.

"Rugby! Of course." Van Dam was delighted. "You always had the impression with John that it could have gone either way: right to the last it was a toss-up — would he build the multi-racial Utopia or play scrum-half for his Province?"

"Exactly." Shuckel was all icy amusement. "In fact, it's probably nearer the mark to say that John turned to politics when he wasn't offered a place in the first team. That's what makes these people so wild. They don't go in for politics because they're really political. They're frustrated. They want action. They want the flamboyant life. Ordinary life is so terrifyingly boring. They're after politics for the same excitement they get in the stands at a Saturday match where it's all sing-alongs and war cries and oranges at half-time and a rough house with the opposition outside the gates after the game. The secret war between the security police and the campus subversives, when you begin to examine it, turns out to be a clumsy farce, not a war at all but a kind of friendly knock-up game between old rivals, the equivalent of Police Reserves against Diggers Thirds."

"But they get arrested, some of them, don't they, Theo?" Mina persisted. "And that's no joke."

"Of course they get arrested. In bloody droves. Or detained or banned or put under house-arrest. Sometimes they go to jail. Yannovitch reckons he could be picked up any time. It depends on the state of play. For instance, there was a chap whom everybody thought non-political, a novice accountant or trainee vet, or something. Anyway, last Sunday afternoon, Wham! His garage goes up in smoke. His old man charged outside to investigate and finds his son has blown off both arms. One at the elbow and the other at the wrist. It turned out that he had this dream of blasting the Voortrekker Monument and had been making a trial run. The cops rolled up, of course. I mean it wasn't easy to hush up something like that. Not with bits of garage, blood and bone sticking to the neighbours' washing. The police took no action. Case in point. This accountant was not going to make any more bombs. So why arrest him? Best leave him as a warning to others. And these are the guys the government calls Communists!''

"What are they then?" Van Dam piped up.

"Anglicans!" Shuckel snapped. "Anglicans with a sort of liberal overlay and Jewish connections. They want the Nationalists to start being nice to natives by letting them into fêtes and jumble sales and so on. That's their earnest wish. Multi-racial niceness. Their fear is the coming blood, the slaughter. Give a little now, right, that's their philosophy, and maybe the blacks won't take it all later.''

"Then why does the government keep calling them Communists?" Mina demanded.

"Ignorance -- mixed with deceitful flattery. Your average radical acts on a political theory which is a mixture of the Book of Common Prayer, *Time Magazine* stories of student riots and the thrill of the crash tackle. Whatever happens in Berkeley happens here - six months later. The students want a Kennedy, you see, floppy haired, in old Levis and sneakers. But what they've got instead is some old white-haired lunatic in *veldskoen*. So they're increasingly pissed off.''

"Are you still a Marxist, Theo?" van Dam asked.

"I want to keep open at least one option. Or risk disappearing along with all the options.''

Van Dam was pretty amused by this, and from the soft explosions I guessed he was slapping his knee. "What! You're a supervisor at the Pass Office, dedicated body and soul and jackboots to keeping the kaffir in line. Some option. You're a *pâté de foie* Marxist who has ratted on his brothers.''

"I've got principles. And what I'm doing is not outside my principles. You're a bloody old woman, van Dam. I can't expect you to understand. I'm working for change. Real change. I have this dream — a multi-racial society. And I'm trying to get it by working directly in the system. I don't talk like the students. I don't live on hope like you wet Liberals — "

"Leave Ricky alone," Mina shrilled.

"He's got no friends left," van Dam taunted.

"Ricky? Ricky! Hell, he sounds like a mongoose, or something." Shuckel gave a bitter snort at his own joke.

"He's a good teacher and twice the man you are. You . . . clerk!"

"Native Affairs *Supervisor*, if you don't mind." Shuckel was clearly stung.

"Never mind Theo's career," van Dam chipped in impatiently, "what about these three Rs? Mary's given us two of them — what's the third? Rugby, revolution and . . . ?"

"Shut up Ricky," Mina said flatly, "can't you see the state she's in?"

I heard Mary's faintly hysterical giggle. "Oh, he's just being kind — you're humouring me, aren't you Ricky? You know what the third R is as well as I do."

I realised from the intense silence that no one particularly liked the third of the three Rs. Mary giggled again. Then I knew what it was about her that sounded so strange. She was drunk.

"Now you've gone and done it," Shuckel moaned. "Now you've set her off. And exactly what do you mean when you say I have no friends?"

"How was I to know what she was thinking of?" Van Dam sounded hurt.

"She thinks of nothing else," Mina retorted.

"It's the drink that brings it on," van Dam said. "As for friends, Theo, the fact is you don't have any since you went to work for the government."

"Oh no? Well, if I don't have any friends, then tell me what we're all doing here together in my car."

"We're not here because we're friends," Mina said. "It's just that we have no one else. So we stick together . . . out of habit."

Mary began singing in a throaty voice: ". . . His knees were like bullets, burning were his eyes — he aimed his great big shooting stick, between my little thighs . . ."

168

"Please, Mary!" Shuckel yelped furiously. "Could you tone it down a bit? I mean, it's not as if it happened yesterday. I'm truly sorry. We're all sorry. But you mustn't drag it up every minute of the day and night. And lay off the hard stuff. It's killing you."

"She drinks to forget," van Dam said.

"Excuse me, but I drink to remember," Mary corrected him affably and began humming to herself.

"Well, you should cut down. Then maybe you'll forget. That's all I can say." Shuckel started the car and revved the engine angrily.

"Oh yes, I like that," Mina hissed derisively. "That's typical of you. It's easy for you to talk. How would you like it if you'd been raped?"

Mary stopped humming. "I want to go home," she announced abruptly.

"There you are — now you've really upset her," Mina accused Shuckel.

"Um, I think, actually, Min, that the boy is waiting for you to finish," van Dam murmured.

"Oh heck," Mina swallowed hard, "I'd forgotten all about him."

"My God! And people wonder why there's a revolution coming," Shuckel growled.

Cup and saucer splashed on to the flooded tray and Shuckel gunned the engine. I wrenched the tripod off the window and jumped. The big back wheels of the Mercedes screeched past my exposed toes, and raced into the night.

I examined my faint reflection in the speckled glass around the serving hatch and decided how silly I'd been, how imbecilic, how pathetic, to have thought for a moment that any one of my old friends might have recognised me. In my flapping tunic, my baggy shorts, my filthy, under-sized sandshoes with the flaps cut out of the toes I was beyond recognition; I was as common as air. I was nothing you could put a name to; I was merely something everyone had around the place, friends might have recognised Harry Moto, but then — I wasn't Harry any longer. I had at last achieved the invisibility I'd so envied in the cleaners at St Bonaventure's, and in those terms I was, or so I thought, a success; I had become, in short, quite simply, "the boy". Unloading dishes

into the kitchen sink I found that it was indeed my lucky
night. In the cold coffee swilling around in the tray I discovered sunken treasure. Shuckel had tipped me sixpence.

Looking back now, I realise what a stupid dream this was,
this hope of invisibility. But there you are: we're all dreamers
here. It's a fatal vice. And what do you think we dream of,
down here in doldrum country, where nothing shifts or alters?
I'll tell you — we dream of change. And the more things stay
the same, the more furiously we dream of things being different. In this fair land, after say, the perpetual motion
machine that runs on water, there is no dream more popular
than change. Political change. Now, there are two types of
change: that which is not allowed (because it is against the
law) and that which is not possible (because it is quite mad).
    The stuff of illegal dreams tends to be pretty dull — multi-
racial lavatories, love across the colour bar, government soup-
kitchens in the shanty towns and so on. Not surprisingly
most people prefer the dreams of the insane. Take old Bruno
Lochner, fierce and flushed, the puckered skin of his cheeks
like a withered peach, darkening into the mottled reds and
ochres of a Bushman wall painting, with a fierce bottle-
brush moustache on which his large nose, pimpled as the finger
of a batting glove, rested the way Kilroy's does on the wall in
schoolboy drawings, founder of Patent Medicine Emporia,
or PAMEP Stores, "Branches in 15 Locations" and one of
Epstein's biggest customers, who dreamed of cities freed
from the huge black townships dumped on their outskirts
to supply labour to white factories, shops and offices and
homes. Lochner's personal vision was of high-speed trains.
He gave most of his money for research into a one-hundred-
and-fifty-miles an hour super express. With such a train, he
told us, it would be possible to move all black workers daily
between the city and their tribal reserves hundreds of miles
away, thus achieving one of the fondest dreams of your
average South African (after a motor car that runs on water),
i.e. purified cities free at last of their "black spots", and
"white by night". The dream came to nothing but it fired
the public imagination and an enterprising toymaker brought
out scale models; they sold like crazy these "Lochner Bullets"
as they were known, in tough plastic, packed with tiny,

extremely realistic models of "workers", and complete with
loading ramps, stations and the characteristic huts of each of
the tribal homelands into which they thundered with their
human freight, and while the craze lasted children could be
seen everywhere, down on their knees in the dust, helping
thousands of workers to commute hundreds of miles between
Pretoria and Mozambique, or Durban and Zululand, Benoni
and the Transkei.

Ralph Swirsky of the Boomplatz Pharmacy was another
dreamer. Along with "Lochner's Bullets" we had "Swirsky's
Fences". You see, old Ralphie's passion was for high-rise
fencing. As everybody knew, he told Epstein, getting Africans
out of the white cities was only half the story: one of the
greatest problems the country faced, besides soil erosion,
was the problem of keeping safely in the Reserves those you
couldn't use. Because so many of them found it difficult to
eat, they were forever getting up and swarming into the
towns in huge numbers settling in locations and shanty-towns
and clogging the servants' quarters of decent suburban houses,
often six or ten to a room, and causing no end of trouble.
Problem: how to keep them down on the farm? Answer, he
told Epstein and me with a triumphant smile in which his
pink, petalled lips trembled in his round, heavy, rather
swarthy face, until a smile was abruptly born, breaking from
the little spit-bubble which habitually formed across his rose-
bud mouth, like a butterfly bursting from the pupa, *the*
answer was barbed wire: "You fence the buggers in!" Even
Epstein, who made a point of buttering up his customers,
couldn't entirely stop himself smiling at that. "Pull the other
one, Ralphie," he said amiably. But it turned out that Swirsky
was very serious; he envisaged thousands of miles of fencing,
twelve foot high, proof against the sharpest wire-cutters and
electrified, criss-crossing the entire country and surrounding
all tribal reserves. He planned to write to the Minister about
his plan. "You do that, old chief," Epstein advised, scarcely
bothering to keep a straight face, "and while you're about it,
do me a big favour and ask him if I can get a permit for a
second garden-boy . . ."

But then, when we came back a few weeks later, Swirsky
showed us this letter from the Minister who said he was very
impressed with the idea and the government was considering

offering tax incentives on the scheme. Next thing, the newspapers had picked up the story, featuring it under headlines like NEW DEAL FOR URBAN AFRICANS, and were sponsoring competitions to find fencing designs based on traditional tribal motifs, so as to be in harmony with the tribal homelands through which fences passed. And there were letters from readers signing themselves "Zuluboy" of Tarkastadt and "Desert Rat" of Cyrildene arguing about the best height for the fence, and barb penetration, optimum gauge, snag rate and the sort of electrical charge it should carry: stun, inhibit, kill or whatever. For weeks people talked of nothing but Swirsky's Fences. Heady times . . .

When the Cottage closed that night, Puffdot gave me an envelope.

"What's this?"

"Your wages — minus breakages. Fifteen and six."

"But my notice isn't worked. There is tomorrow night. I'm not finished."

"You're finished as from now," Puffdot said.

"I hoped we might work out the Peeping Tom misunderstanding."

"Well, we might have done. Only this isn't anything to do with your little accident. I might have been prepared to overlook that. But I can't overlook politics. What you believe about this country is your business. Still, and all, I'm having no bloody agitators here. I'm running a roadhouse not a commie cell. Not that I've got anything against change. I believe it will come. Must come. But not in our lifetime. Meantime, I'm not harbouring no bloody dangers to the State."

At that point, Joerie and Jacko wandered over and lounged pointedly on the counter on the other side of the serving hatch.

I made one last appeal. "Look at me. Do I look like a danger to the State?"

To do him justice, he seemed doubtful.

"Go on, trust your own eyes. What possible harm could I do to anyone? Why do you think it is that people won't leave me alone, Mr Puffdot? All I want is to be left alone. To be lost. Forgotten. But there's always someone after me. Why is that?"

172

Again, to be fair, he thought this over. He really tried. Then he said, "Look Harry, don't think you're special for being singled out. Tell me who they aren't after?" Then I knew that though he looked at me, and believed his eyes, what he really saw wasn't his tray-collector; he saw the two men in the grey Chev who had called on him earlier in the evening after I'd taken my drive with Koosie, and behind the two men, he saw the famous, terrifying Dekker.

"He's not a danger to nobody," Joerie said positively.

"Except to young girls out for a bit of slap and tickle," said Jacko.

"Except to your plates and cups and saucers, Mr Puffdot," Joerie added.

"I've docked the breakages from his wages, don't you worry about that," Puffdot said irritably. "Now let the boy clear off without any more funny comments from you smart-arses."

Jacko stared hard at me and laughed. "He's not a danger," he repeated deliberately, "he's just a randy young bugger who catches his thrills by peeping at white girls' boobies." And he and Joerie clutched each other hysterically.

A metallic mist seemed to rise out of the zinc counter between me and the laughing waiters. I went cold, then hot, and I had a curious singing inside my head above my right eye. I remember I reached out across the counter very carefully and took hold of Joerie's lank, yellow hair. With all the grease in it, I felt I was pushing my fingers into warm, wet grass and I was obliged to turn my wrist sharply so as to lock into the hair and pull it up into a kind of Chinese top-knot which wore my fist as a cruel, white-knuckled brooch. I yanked abruptly and with a yelp Joerie slid across the polished counter as easily as a loaded tray. Jacko reached after him, stuttering with fury. As he did so Puffdot lifted a huge hand and brought it down on his back as if he were swatting a fly and Jacko, frightfully winded, lay thrashing on the counter beside Joerie, tears streaming down his cheeks but, game little fellow to the last, still coughing curses. Joerie said nothing at all but gazed up at me with big eyes and a little spit in the corner of his mouth. Puffdot leaned over and took him by the scruff of the neck and looked at me bleakly but not unkindly.

"Best be going, Harry. I'll hold these two till you're clear. Run and fetch your push-bike."

"I'm sorry about this."

"Same here, Mata Hari. Reckon you've got enough on your plate without having an assault charge to face. Get out now. A man should have a chance. It's pretty black out there. Get on your bike and pedal like hell. Hope to lose yourself somewhere." And with his chin, he nodded me into the night.

13

Puffdot didn't let me change. To get out and keep going had been his most insistent advice. In his dreadful eagerness to see the back of me he insisted I keep my collector's uniform — as a "going-away present". Big deal. I was pretty sure the cops were waiting for me back at my room in Melkbos Street, unless the old place had seen its chance and dropped the last of its collapsing walls on the pack of them. I put my head down and pedalled into the night with scarce a backward glance and terrible anticipation in my heart. Little Glass Heidi waved her branched hand from her roof-top perch. I waved back. As if disapproving of this fraternisation Puffdot switched her off. I guessed he would have watched me go from the fake upstairs Cottage windows with their stapled, cardboard bows and sighed hugely. The men in the Chev would be satisfied.

Moments later, I began to cry. But I didn't even slow down. I tell you there is nothing more difficult than coping with a sobbing fit on a bike. I had to wipe my nose on the short sleeves of my flat-boy's tunic and it wasn't really satisfactory. There is nothing more ridiculous than a weeping cyclist.

I reached the stretch of road out beyond the Belgravia Traffic Circle where the tar unfolds for about half a mile in a gentle downward slope and you can just about make out the red flare of the city on the horizon, when I heard the car behind me. I knew who it must be. The men in the Chev weren't going to wait until I got home. It made sense. If they took me out then, I'd never be heard of again. So what else is new? After all, I'd never been heard of again once *already* when I'd left home for Raboobie. They'd just be making it official. Granted I made a show of defiance. Stood up to pedal, put on speed, helped by the slope. But in my heart I knew if I'd a white flag I would've waved it. The car closed in and its bright lights lit me up, snivelling, jangling and flapping, like I was the Union Buildings. I could hear the engine pumping at what sounded like inches from my rattling back mudguard. I turned around. Now that was a big mistake. The sort of mistake only someone like Lot's wife would really appreciate. And like her I paid the price. Dazzled by the headlights, I swerved and fell.

I lay on the gravel shoulder of the roadside, slowly mixing a grainy porridge of blood and sand in my mouth. I seemed to have come down on my chin, but apart from perhaps a bitten tongue or loose teeth, I was passably whole. I watched my back wheel spinning, spokes mashing up the moonlight like an egg-beater. The car made a U-turn and stopped in front of me with its lights blazing. I tried to shield my eyes. I had an idea that this was how old Saul must have felt out on the Damascus Road when the big illumination hit him. And then a voice spoke from beyond the lights: "It's me Harry, Mary!"

I found myself praying: "Harry Mary, full of grace . . . " I got up slowly, feeling for breakages, wiping my eyes and nose and mouth on my tunic sleeve. It came away bloody. Nose, I thought, nose and lips maybe. I picked up my bike. It gave a sad shiver and a little rattle. I tried to shake some life into it, but the front wheel died on me with a rusty gasp of tyre against tin mudguard.

"I thought you were dead, Harry."

"I am dead."

She got out of the car and came over to me. I gave the front wheel a last, desperate push but it panted and wheezed like a bloody asthmatic. Mary fished out a large handkerchief and dabbed at my face.

"You upper lip is split and you have a nose-bleed. Can you walk?"

She drove fast. Well enough, but rather angrily. I couldn't see her face very clearly. But she seemed as pretty as ever. I noticed she kept muttering under her breath. When she wasn't saying something to me, she was talking furiously to herself. And then there was this terrible laugh. She had a

176

wild, nervous laugh that shattered the conversation, rising and falling like a cock-crow.

"I'm glad you came back. I felt so sure it was you. But in that funny outfit — well, you see lots of them about, but you never expect to know the person inside, somehow." And her clarion shriek ripped through the dark.

"I haven't come back. This is an accident. You bumped into me, that's all. I'm actually miles away, really."

"Kenny Darling, he's a priest now, you know. He thought you were dead. He offered Masses for the repose of your soul."

"My soul's O.K. It's the rest of me I worry about. How are you?"

"Oh, I'm fine. I go off my head every now and then. But otherwise I'm all right."

"Where do you want to go?"

"Anywhere we can be quiet and talk. Your place, if you like."

"Not my place."

She glanced at me. "I'd take you to my flat, only I don't think you'd like it — I'm on the tenth floor. We'd have to use the lift."

"It's the uniform, isn't it?"

"I'm afraid so. We have a nightwatchman, you see, who stands guard at the lift doors. He'd go mad if I came home with a flat-boy. I think we'd better go somewhere private."

We ended up at the Municipal Reservoir on the outskirts of the white suburbs. Known as Lovers' Lake it was the only decent stretch of water the city could boast. Surrounded by weeping willows and green lawns set in flanking woods of bluegums. In the centre of the lake, a fountain sprayed plumes of water high into the air, lit by fierce green and pink lights set into the base. The lake was the place lovers went when they wanted to be alone. Everyone went there when they wanted to be alone. The result was that, after midnight, the spaces between the willows and the bluegums were packed with the sort of solid, gleaming mass of cars you might have expected at a Saturday night drive-in. Mary piloted us expertly among the silent cars, their windows fogged with the hot, excited breath of the late-night lovers, and backed the Mini into a handy space between the bulging trunks of two huge bluegums. She switched off the engine and leaned back in her seat, her face changing colours with the light from the fountain.

"Is there anything I can do, Harry?"

"I'm beyond help, I'm afraid."

She nodded calmly. "I know what you mean. I'm like that, too. Ruined. Beyond salvation. It's been that way ever since my attack. I suppose you heard them talking about my attack tonight." She reached over, opened the glove compartment and pulled out a half-jack: "Voddies?" I got the impression she wasn't sorry when I refused. "Relax Harry," she patted my bare knee. "I won't keep you. Did you hear about the assault?"

"I do seem to remember some mention of it when I was waiting on you. You sang a song."

She nodded. "When the subject comes up, I get around to singing . . . providing I've had enough of this," She tilted the half-jack and took another swig.

"I'd never thought of you as a singer, really."

"Times change. I never thought of you as a flat-boy. We're none of us who we were. Still, you know how you used to complain that nothing ever happened here? Well, something happened to me. I should feel grateful."

"You mean your attack?"

"I suppose so. But I don't really like to talk about it."

"Fine," I said. 'Well, that suits me."

"I was with a boy, Harrison Ford, perhaps you remember him?"

"I thought you didn't like to talk about it?"

"I don't. But I find I talk about it most of the time. My rape was probably the major event in my young life. It made an impression." She took several giant swallows of vodka.

"Harrison Ford, the swimmer?"

"The same."

"Backstroke was his strong point." I remembered him, a shining hero just out of the water after yet another great win in the school gala, muscles like gold braid.

"Butterfly, actually. It's a very demanding stroke."

"He was always a powerful brute, Harrison Ford."

"So we always thought," Mary nodded with the steady, heavy concentration, the wide-eyed sincerity of the newly

178

drunk. "But surprise, surprise, surprise, on the night, where was our man of steel then? When this monster broke the car window, opened the door and waved his knife and began pulling me out of the car I screamed a bit, and tried to grab hold of Harrison. He seemed rather disinterested and I simply couldn't think why. You can imagine my surprise, as I was dragged kicking and screaming and hearing my clothes tearing, a terrible sound, when I looked back and saw Harrison stretched out in his seat. He'd fainted clean away."

"Who attacked you?"

"Well, there's the problem. You see, I still don't know. My eyes were shut most of the time and with Harrison, the only witness, out like a light, well, no one knows for sure — but they think it was the panga man. But as the panga man usually knifes his victims in the process, some people thought this man was a cheap imitator. But according to the police surgeon, who examined me afterwards, he'd done a fairly good job."

"It must have chewed up your people."

"My mother died some years ago, and Daddy — you remember Daddy? — well, he was delighted. Absolutely thrilled. You see, for him the long years of waiting were over at last. For his sake I was almost pleased about it — if you can understand what I mean. In the last year he'd become very much worse with his guns and his phobias. He'd a pistol, sometimes two in every room and he'd taken to absolutely haunting the police auctions where they get rid of the dogs that don't come up to scratch. Usually that meant they were too wild to be trained, or too mad, or too mean, and he'd buy them, starve them and let them roam the grounds at night. Well, what with the searchlights he had mounted on the roof, the trip wires on the lawn, the dogs howling at the barbed wire, the continual false alarms when Daddy would tear outside and begin blazing away with his shotgun, the neighbours forever complaining, life was hell. But it all stopped on the night I was raped. I'll never forget it. I came in from the police station and Daddy was waiting up for me. I could tell by his face that he was worried. He'd been through this before — for years and years he'd waited for the moment, hoping against hope. When he caught sight of my torn dress, I saw the faintest gleam in his eye, instantly quenched — there'd been too many false alarms and Daddy was being careful. The he saw the policeman and he knew something really had happened at last." Mary smiled fondly at the memory and pulled at the vodka bottle. "He listened very quietly to the policeman's story. Then he went outside and spoke to Phineas — d'you remember Phineas, our night-watchman? Well, Phineas was in charge of the dogs. He had to starve them and to let them loose at night in the garden and then, what was much harder, he had to catch them in the morning again and lock them away for the day all slavering and even hungrier. There's something about Dobermans, they slaver an awful lot — and bite, of course, constantly. They bit Phineas all the years we had him — anyway, as I was saying, Daddy went outside and got hold of Phineas and took him to the top of the garden and pointed into the darkness where we could hear the dogs wailing and he said, quite simply: 'Feed them.' That's all, just 'Feed them.' Well, then old Phineas broke down. It was so moving." She drained the last of the vodka, smacked her lips and then without a word she opened her door and stepped into the dark. I watched her walk down to the edge of the lake and pitch the bottle with all her might into the water where it caught the fountain lights briefly and sank.

The night outside thickened and darkened. A couple of cars nearby started up and pulled out, unsheathing head-lights, flashing like knives across the black water. Then the fountain was switched off; the last plumes of spray stood a moment in the sky then crashed and rose no more. The streaming base of the fountain stood exposed, poking ab-surdly out of the lake, old, wet, ugly. I had no watch but I knew it must be very late. Mary climbed in beside me, shivering a little and humming something I recognised as the tune of the song I'd heard her singing at the Roadhouse.

"I'm sorry, Mary."

"No need. In my father's terms, I'm a success. I made it at last."

"It was an accident. It could have happened to anyone."

"Maybe," she said softly. "Maybe it was an accident to start with. But now I reckon it's a career. Do you understand what I mean? Just waiting around for the next time."

"Listen," I said, "who better to understand you? That's

the story of my life. An accident that turned out to be a career."

She took my hand. "Harry, I'm so pleased to see you again."

"Please don't be. This isn't really me; you're seeing a figure from the past, a ghost. You're looking at a ghost. I've vanished from the life you remember. No one else can see me. I've been closer to old friends than I am to you now and they've looked straight through me."

She leaned across to me and pressed her face into my neck and gave what I thought was a giggle until I felt the wetness and knew she was crying. "But I knew you, Harry. Instantly. Remember, I have an eye for your disguises. The last time we saw each other you were in disguise. The night of the dance, remember?"

"No," I said as firmly as I could, "I don't remember."

She nestled closer and we sat in silence for a while hearing the little oily waves lapping among the reeds. I thought she'd gone to sleep when she said: "I forget things all the time since my attack. I'm not very well, Harry. I get depressed and forget things. And I drink."

"And then what happens?"

"I get even more depressed but it helps me to remember. Of course the others don't approve. I don't approve myself."

"What are the others doing now?"

"Yannovitch is an anarchist. Rick van Dam and Mina are both teachers . . . and Mina is pregnant by Rick. Jack Wyner we hardly ever see. He's an articled clerk in an accountant's office and is in love with a girl called Hilda, a very tall girl with a lot of money. They go away to her beach cottage in Plettenberg Bay and always dine al fresco there, he tells me. She is very keen on his buying a baby Jag. It's a sign of success, she says, a man's first baby Jag."

"And Shuckel works for the Department of Native Affairs — that's an odd step for a man with radical opinions."

"He says it's a logical move. He says he's carrying the fight to the enemy. It doesn't make any sense to me but in the mad world of politics perhaps he is right. To be effective you have to be more insane than they are." She slipped a warm hand inside my tunic. "How are the old breasts?"

"Filling out."

I had a go at loosening her hand but she twisted my chest hairs around her finger.

"Do you go out with Shuckel?" My voice had a squeaky edge to it.

"I wouldn't say that. But I sleep with him on and off. It's a great comfort. But it's not quite the same thing as going out with him, is it?"

"I really ought to be moving on."

She nodded. "I know. Your chest is really hairy. It wasn't like that last time, back-stage at the school dance, all those lifetimes ago." She gave a delighted, rather drunken giggle. "How stupid we must have looked when Brother — what was his name?"

"Donally."

" — When Brother Donally burst in on us." Her grip tightened more painfully still. "The swine! To spy on us. To lord it over us the way he did. To revel in his power to terrify us; to turn me into a hopeless, snivelling baby; to send you away . . ."

"But he didn't send me away. I went. It seemed the thing to do. I'm sorry."

"If he were here now I'd know what to do. I'd kill him. Damn school days!"

"Oh school," I babbled, "of course, *school*. God, I haven't thought about St Bonaventure's for ages." And I tried to pry loose her terrible grip.

Then, at last, she really laughed and her fingers relaxed. "My God, Harry, but you *have* been dead a long time . . . It's gone. Well, what there was left of it. Sold. Every bog and byre, jot and tittle, flogged to the Dragon. Bought by the government as a site for a new experimental farm for the Afrikaans University. I don't know how they deconsecrated the chapel — probably spat three times on the whore of Rome and gave three cheers for Calvin. Anyway it's gone. The buildings are still there, of course, but the place is swarming with learner farmers in khaki shorts and shaven heads who tear around the place in tractors and beat-up Volkswagens swopping stories about yields per acre, or what happened at Nagmaal, or gossiping about Army training. They've ploughed up the playing fields and sown strains of wonder wheat. The quad is full of strange grasses. There are harvesters in the bike sheds, pigs in the armoury, there's lucerne on the tennis courts, manure in the swimming pool and in the old school hall where you and I swung effortlessly among the dancers all that time ago, battery hens are pecking at their bars."

It should not have shocked me. But it did. "I really should be making tracks."

She lifted my tunic clear up to my shoulders. "My, but your breasts really have filled out." And she kissed my right nipple.

"Honestly, I have to go."

"A little longer," she pleaded. "no one knows you're here."

"I had a secret life," I said, "no one knew where I was. Or who I was. That's all changed. People are crowding me. All I have going for me is that I'm just ahead of them. For now. It's not that I'm not pleased to see you. I really am. But I can't stay, you see. You do see, don't you, Mary?"

She nodded. "Of course. It's dangerous for you to stay. Go then, whenever you like." And she wrapped both arms tightly around my neck.

I kissed her. It seemed the best thing to do. She pushed me away, but gently. I thought I'd done the wrong thing, that an experienced observer seeing me then would have said, "Stuff me, but this boy knows *nothing!*" I'm just on the point of actually apologising, for God's sake, when she sits bolt upright and, reaching behind her, unzips her dress, unhooks her bra and carrying it on one finger, drops it onto the back seat. Barely time to see the breasts of my dreams swinging by, powdered with moonlight, before she pulls my head down, nuzzling the nape of my neck and sending her tongue into my ear, soft, pink, wet and quick as a tiny jackhammer. I held onto her breasts for dear life. Who says dreams don't come true? But, crazily polite to the last, I gave her the option of waking me.

"Are you sure this is really what you want to do?"

"Come on, I've never made love to a ghost." Her hands were working at my pants. She pushed them down. "Ah, why do I get the feeling that I've been here before?" She stroked me. "Poor Harry." She lay back on an armrest. "Now, me," she commanded, and obligingly lifted herself inches above the seat. "For old time's sake."

And there I was, easing her pants over her knees, elbows going in every direction. All action, I was, doing everything but running on the spot, while she seemed to be lying back and watching, cool, calm, one step ahead. I snagged her pants on her shoes where they tore but she laughed and kicked them into the back seat, and pulled me down onto her, cutting off my apologies. "Now Harry, quickly," and she took me in her hand and drove me inside her, breathing in my ear with a steady rhythm until she felt I had the idea and then she dropped away, sighing beneath me, fell away again and again and I followed her down until the Mini was rocking in time to us with little squeaks, though whether they came from the car springs or from her I could not say until it was too late and Mary covered her mouth with her hands and the cries stopped. Meanwhile I went on, caught in the speeding rhythm of my own breathing, until the car seemed suddenly to blow up like a balloon and explode, raining down pieces into nowhere.

How we ever managed it, alongside the steering wheel, above the hand-brake, I'll never know. Very slowly, feeling began to return to my toes which I found to be braced against the armrest. Under my finger tips was the grooved stitching of the seat cover. The window had steamed up and seemed to cut off every outside sound except for a soft tapping. A tree branch, I decided. It was then, lying so quietly we might have been asleep, that we heard the voices. The tapping was suddenly louder. Mary froze and I felt myself shrink and fall from her. Cold crept between us, making us wet and separate where we'd been so warm together. I opened the driver's window an inch or two. Mary sat up, smoothing her dress across her knees, beginning this broken-voiced whimper as shadows appeared from nowhere and moved across the windscreen. Then a white, furry ball of light leaped in the foggy windows. A torch. Mary wept: "No, no, no!"

What looked like a wet, black beak poked through my open window and a big, strong voice, calculated to broadcast across the thirty acres that made up the ground of the Municipal Reservoir and reach all the other lovers parked round about under the bluegums and hidden in knotty darkness, bellowed its disbelief: "Hey Mannetjies, come look what we got here! ''

A second beak rested on the window. The torch light swept again. "My God, Sarge!" said the one called Mannetjies, "It's a bloody flat-boy — on the job!"

"Help us!" Mary shrilled. Then she whispered harshly in my ear. "Leave this to me. It's the panga man. This time I'm fighting back."

I was struggling with my pants. "No, no, it's the police."

"Believe me, Harry. This has happened before. I know. I remember it all. He has a weak point. He can be lured. But stay close."

Somebody opened the door and an arm decked with sergeant's stripes yanked me out.

"Harry, don't leave me!"

I got angry and pushed the sergeant in the chest. He hit me very hard on the side of the head and I fell over. I spat grass. "Making love isn't against the law!"

"Of course not," said the sergeant, "but we prefer you to do it at home."

"That's right," said the one called Mannetjies, "and you're supposed to stick to your own kind."

"Any other way is immorality," said the sergeant.

I got up and leaned against the door jam. "Take it easy with the girl. She's been attacked once before."

"You're telling me," the sergeant waved briskly to Mary who held her dress primly up to her neck, "Come on lady. Out!"

Mary let her dress fall, and leaned back, offering her breasts. "Come and get me," she said.

His eyes bulged with disbelief. Then he reached for her. I heard him scream. The next thing I knew he was on the grass at my feet with his hands to his face and I didn't know what he was trying to tell me until I saw the blood between his fingers, dark purple, almost black in the moonlight, and I realised then why she'd wanted him close. She'd gone for his eyes. And the demented rooster's triumphant cackle shook the darkness.

14

They sat me in a cell painted a thick creamy enamel, beginning to yellow, and harshly reflecting the overhead bulb, locked into a wire basket set in the high ceiling. A metal table bolted to the floor carried a Gideon Bible. Two bunkbeds, sporting scratchy, blue-striped mattresses, hung from the wall on metal arms. A washbasin, missing its plug, stood under the window and in the corner was a white enamel pail, chipped blue-black around the rim and a box of government-issue lavatory paper. Some would have called it bleak, the crusted bars across the window, the green steel door and stone black floor. Some would have called it bloody inhospitable. But there you are — after the terrible excitement of the arrest, bringing grim memories of Brother Donally's attack after the school dance, I didn't mind being left alone.

A huge constable, Pielletjies by name, said to me before he locked me away, "This here's called 'reception', O.K? Here's where you can think about your sins till I come for you."

"How is the girl?"

"Don't worry. Seems this has happened before."

"Arrested before?"

"No man, raped."

All my time in the cells at Main Street Police Station they kept me waiting in "reception".

Truly, my life has not been one of unequalled progress. When I was first in there, before I saw the place as my home, I was very nervous. Even in Koosie's Big Hotel, it seemed I wasn't destined to get past the foyer.

That cell was so quiet, filled with the long-drawn hush

which sounds when you hold a shell to your ear and is no sound at all really, but the ear listening to its own silence. My tension expressed itself in a specific physical symptom. When the cops attacked Mary and me my sphincter went into spasm and the old buttocks, ever unreliable in a crisis, locked tighter than those suction cups opposing teams of horses were shown struggling to pull apart in the section on "The Vacuum" in my school science book. In an attempt to relax, I began my chest exercises. I wanted to keep them really quiet. I think I managed, to begin with at least. But the softest whisper bounced around the white, electric spaces of my cell. I soon discovered that if I broke my puffs by clicking my tongue it sounded grand. Before I knew it I was tapping my feet, breathing deeper and slapping my knees, playing a complicated tarradiddle as I bounced and swayed. I couldn't stop. I was an engine, a pneumatic drill, an orchestra playing a symphony of percussion: tap heel and toe, slap knee and bounce, breathe, puff-puff, and bounce again. I was tambourines, my cheeks clashing cymbals, my chest a kettle-drum. I went on until my head spun and I had to rest. Let's face it, maybe I had no natural sense of rhythm, but I was a real trier. When I was tired of giving things a bash, I sang; I sang *"Binga, banga, bonga, I don't wanna leave the Congo . . "* It was the song I'd been singing in the back of the police van to cover the sound of Mary's screams.

During the arrest the frightened couples parked around us began, at the first glimpse of the police, taking off in hundreds, racing each other around the bluegums, everyone fighting and jockeying to be first out of the gate. A few brave souls stayed to gawk at Mary's slobbering victim. The sight of her spitting and half-naked caused a great stir. She was overpowered at last by Mannetjies, trying desperately not to look at her breasts but keeping a sharp eye on her hooked nails, and he managed to get her into the back of the police van and handcuffed her to the wire grill protecting the cab window. The sound of the engine made her wilder still. She bucked, spat and kicked until the steel walls of the van were booming like a coming thunderstorm, jerking at her handcuffs as if she'd willingly tear her arms out. I edged along the seat, calling her name very gently, telling myself how they said it worked with horses. When I was really close,

I dropped into the Congo song: *"They have things like the atom bomb, so I think I'll stay where I om . . ."* I crooned soothingly. It seemed to help. At least she stopped screaming and fell back in the corner shivering. But when I pushed my luck and reached out a hand and touched her shoulder she dipped her head like a striking snake and sunk her teeth into my hand and I beat a pretty swift retreat. She loved this and began shrieking again: *"Police-panga! Police-panga!"* in a wild, delighted voice and it was clear she had fixed in her poor, injured mind the belief that the arrival of the police had been a repeat of the first attack on her — only this time she had got her revenge, she had nabbed her man. Through the thick mesh across the window of the driver's cab I made out her victim writhing in his seat, his hands pressed to his blind eyes, weeping blood. Mary grinned like a gargoyle. In her feverish imagination all her attackers were one now: Brother Donally, the second-rate Panga man, the police sergeant. And as far as she was concerned she'd triumphed at last. She'd hit back with a vengeance. And, worst of all, with that savage nip she told me that I was now included among those tormentors.

I waited a long time to meet Dekker. This, I see now, was the softening-up period. I met his men first: two uniformed constables, ou Neels, dapper, with a Clark Gable moustache, sleek as a seal in his specially tailored uniform: he had a tame tailor in Koelietown, he told me, and Pielletjies, a man mountain with his face, as it were, hewn from the rocky peak. Pielletjies was incredibly sloppy, his tunic stained by runnels of food, the overspills of gargantuan meals, and streaked with white, rather chalky, deposits of what I decided was old toothpaste. But a pious soul, less deadly than the polished Neels, always genially reminding me that God would rot my soul in hell one day. My salvation lay in "the good book" he said and he'd bang me on the head with the Gideon Bible before ordering me onto my knees for prayer and then creeping out of my cell while I buried my splitting head in my arms pretending to call on God to strike me down for the sinner I was, watching him leave. From the rear he was even bigger, his rumpled pants hanging in deep swinging creases like the baggy skin of an elephant's hindquarters.

"You pray real good, Harry," he said approvingly.

"It's only natural. I spent my schooldays on my knees."

"You're going to need every prayer you pray."

"Why are you keeping me here?"

"You're going to see Mr Dekker," ou Neels smirked, "and have a chat about your life and times. He's got a big interest in you."

"But why?"

"That's for him to know and you to say."

It was Pielletjies and ou Neels who prepared the clumsy, horrid little surprise I found in my cell when I woke up one morning. It was exactly their crude touch. Hanging from the window bars was a rag doll with stringy black hair, a pyjama cord knotted around its neck. Someone had taken the trouble to paint the face, rather clumsily, a dirty brown colour, rather similar to mine. Otherwise there was no resemblance. When I woke the next morning the doll was there still. After that I lost track of the days of the week. But mostly it felt like Sunday. Sundays at home in the old days started with Church and ended with the Epilogue on the radio with nothing in between. I prayed a lot in my cell — Pielletjies saw to that — with nothing in between.

"One day, Harry, my old mate," Yannovitch used to tell me when we lay around Jack Wyner's pool on Sundays, so bored that even the sight of puffy white clouds trawling their shadows across the lawn was a big event, "when I'm older, y'know, I'm gonna open a special cinema up there on the Ridge, Sundays only."

"Saphead," said van Dam, the optimist, "they're not allowed on Sunday. Nothing moves on Sunday."

"As everybody knows," Yannovitch went on, as if he hadn't heard, "they can't show movies on Sundays. So O.K. I won't load film on the projector."

"And all you'll get is a flickering white light on the screen," van Dam crowed.

"But it moves, doesn't it, this light? And it's white, too. What more can you ask? I tell you, they'll be fighting to get in. Sneer away, van Dam. But one day when you're still a wheeltapper's apprentice and I'm driving my fat yacht around the Bahamas, don't come crying to me."

The policemen Pielletjies and ou Neels were babes in comparison with Dekker's hard men, Lubavitch and Stokkies. First thing they did was to remove my steel arch supports and laces. My sandshoes fell off my feet. I tried marching around my cell barefoot but the pain got so bad I took to my bunk and waved my useless shoes in their faces.

They threw up their hands. "We know, we know. But it's regulations, see? No equipment allowed in the cells except what's provided by the Department of Prisons. Besides, it's not as if you're going anywhere. But of course, if you were to say *something*, to make a statement, then perhaps we could work a point."

I pointed to my bare feet.

"On those cold stones without shoes, you'll get chilblains," was all they said.

"I want to know about the girl. How is she?"

Stokkies grinned. "Foaming."

"What do you expect," Lubavitch demanded, "after she's been raped by a flat-boy."

"I'm not a flat-boy."

Stokkies inclined his head as if graciously accepting the denial. "Then what are you, Harry? And exactly what are you doing here?"

"What sort of question's that? I could ask the same of you."

"You have got lots of cheek," Lubavitch said admiringly. He reached out a hand and took my cheek between thumb and forefinger and twisted until my eyes watered. "That's a question we can easily answer. We're here to learn. You're going to teach us Harry. We think you've got so much to give."

Pielletjies, ou Neels, Lubavitch and Stokkies all came with me on the day I was taken to see the terrible Mr Dekker. They were in a very good mood, humming and skipping alongside me as I marched down a long corridor. They were like kids off to a Sunday school picnic, a sort of end of term treat for good behaviour. The only thing that upset them was my refusal to put my shoes on. I looked, said Stokkies, just like a farm native. We went into a big office painted government green, smelling of musty files and

Cobra floor polish, where a big man lounged on the far side of a big brown desk, tipped back in a swivel chair, feet in the top drawer reading something called *Naught for Your Comfort* by one Trevor Huddleston. He was working his way steadily through a bag of nuts, tossing the shells into the wastepaper basket behind his right shoulder. His white shirt was open at the neck presenting a few reddish chest hairs. His face was full and beefy, the skin, thin and shining the way you see it on sausages, stretched over the meat beneath. The constable coughed twice before he looked up. His hair was coarse, springy, rather like mine in fact. He marked his place with a little piece of shell, leaned back with what sounded like a happy sigh and patted his Trevor Huddleston.

"I can recommend this book, ou Neels. There's no doubt our natives in the locations are not well off. As policemen we've got to know how they live, on what the Americans call, 'the other side of the tracks'. Do you read much ou Neels?"

"No, Mr Dekker. Only *Detective* and sometimes books like *Gek* and *Dolly*." The constable looked embarrassed.

"Those aren't books, ou Neels. Those are what we call picture stories. And crappy ones at that. Remember, we're in the front line. Pounding beat is all very well, but there's some things you get only from books. And you know what they say, ou Neels: knowledge is power."

Dekker waved me further forward. "Come here little friend. Don't be frightened. My name is Dekker. But you can call me sir." I remembered Koosie's parting gift to me. It was time for a good cringe. I crooked my left knee, dropped my left shoulder and swung side on towards Dekker, bruising my hip on the edge of the desk. My eyes began to water and I lifted my arm up in front of my face. Didn't want him to think I was crying. The move went badly, what with me losing my balance and staggering about and this unsettled the constable who swore and pulled out his pistol.

Dekker waved him away, "Put it down, man, this isn't a shooting gallery. Our little friend is trying to be respectful, I think. And I like a man who knows how to show respect. Point is — has he had words with you boys yet? Have we, as it were, heard his story from his own lips?"

Ou Neels and Pielletjies looked very embarrassed and said nothing.

"He's given us nothing — except a bit of cheek," Luba-vitch admitted.

"He claims he hasn't got anything to tell us we don't know," ou Neels explained.

"But there's no end to what he can tell us!" Dekker exclaimed, tossing his book into a corner and standing up, his eyes shining. He pointed a shaking finger at me. "This boy is a link, a living link between separate but equal races, he is a unique specimen, he straddles the white and the non-white worlds. This boy — " he came over and banged me on the head, such was his excitement — "started off life as white as wedding lace and ended up as some kind of kaffir and thereby, as they say, hangs a tale. It's very important that you tell us everything. Help me and perhaps I can help you."

"I've got nothing to say. You've terrified everyone I know these past months. What more could I tell you?"

Dekker sighed. "Please try to understand — we've spoken to people who've known you, yes, and yes, they have been tremendously helpful in explaining to us what they thought of you and explaining the odd case you are. Some had to overcome the initial reluctance. Naturally I made clear how desperately vital this information was. They understood me. They talked to me. I know *what* you have been. But I still don't understand why!"

"You mean that you frightened the life out of them."

"No, no, no." Dekker shook his head and when he looked at me his grey eyes were shining with sincerity. "All I did was to tell them how much I appreciated their help and how ignorant I was and how I looked to them for — well, for illumination . . . d'you see? Look at it from my point of view. Here is a boy who starts life in a good home, at a fine school, who all of a sudden disappears and goes underground among the Indians in Koelietown, associates with criminals and political agitators from the Native Locations, disappears again and then turns up driving for a Jewish salesman in skin lightening creams who has been instrumental in corrupting the foremost male members of a staunchly religious country town who suddenly begin poking every black woman they meet . . . said boy ducks out of sight again and pops up in a roadhouse collecting trays and there gets a reputation for

192

spying on naked white women and also renews acquaintance with one Koos Mafeteng, a flyboy from the townships, wanted in connection with the murder of a Bantu fruit seller down by the non-European station and known political anarchist who has since fled the country, and then our hero is finally caught interfering with a sick girl late at night in a lonely spot. We looked through your room in Maharaj Mansions. Nothing came to light, I'm sorry to say. We spoke to your parents. Your Mom wasn't much help, between you and me, because she started crying as soon as your name came up and didn't stop. All your Dad would say was that he was sure you must be fine, otherwise he'd have read about it in the papers. Here, look at this." He passed me a photograph. It was the shot the policeman Donald had got of Koosie and me on the day I went to University. "Despite evidence of old friendship even Mafeteng wasn't keen to talk about you, Harry. Why's that?"

"What about the girl — Mary? She'll have talked to you."

But Dekker shook his head sadly. "She's no help at all. You see, Miss Smithson has gone a step further, she's forgotten you ever existed."

"Where is she?"

"In care, I told you, the girl is sick. The sergeant she attacked lost an eye, by the way. But we won't touch her. We don't punish the sick. We're not barbarians." He got up and signalled the others. Lubavitch and Stokkie, ou Neels and Pielletjies came over. Like rugby forwards they put their arms around each other and stood in front of me. I was surrounded by the front row of a scrum. "Don't you feel anything for your country, Harry?"

"What country?" I looked around.

"Did you know," Pielletjies persisted, "that there are Russian submarines off the Pondoland coast?"

Dekker stuck a thumb out. I wondered briefly if he was going for an eye-gouge. "See that? My thumb is covered with callouses. Great horny buggers they are, too." He held his hand up to the light turning it this way and that so I'd get a better look at the knobbled ridge running from the fleshy V along the inside of his thumb to the tip, scaly little hemispheres with a pinkish tinge, the leathery skin split, peeling the way old cricket balls do. "You ask people overseas, or the English language press, priests, the bloody Afro-Asian bloc at UNO, or any other bunch of pinko-liberals where I got these callouses and they'll say it was too much trigger action. They'll tell you I grew 'em shooting kaffirs!" He opened his mouth and from it came something that began as a laugh and ended in a phlegmy cough. His fingers danced for a moment among the line of pen tops in his tunic pocket before he settled on a blue ball-point. He yanked it out and held it over his head. "Well, here's my gun!" He was shouting and waving the pen in the air. "Would you believe that I grew 'em by pushing a pen! It may come as a surprise to you to know that I don't hold with shooting kaffirs out of hand."

"Please!" I assured him desperately. "I believe you."

"You see, we're not animals," Dekker said.

"Not Frankensteins," ou Neels added and pushed his hands back into his pockets.

"Remember that, Harry, when you get out into the world again and they dish up all that claptrap about the police. We're not murderers." Dekker shook his head really hard.

"Not Nazis," ou Neels said.

"I mean, it's not us who makes the laws," Pielletjies shouted. "We're just the guys who got to pick up the shit!"

"You talked about helping me — a deal . . . perhaps?"

Dekker nodded solemnly. "Give me your story. Every detail and in your own words. Don't care how long it takes. Reel it off and someone will write it down. Tray simple — not so, ou Neels?"

"Tray bong," ou Neels nodded.

"That's French," Pielletjies said proudly.

"Where did you learn to speak French?"

"We had a Mauritian in here a while back. He'd been blowing up electricity pylons," Lubavitch said. "We picked up a fair smattering of froggy."

"You live and learn. It's never too late," Dekker said. "We can make a deal. Sure. But I want every detail, however petty it may seem, with names, addresses, dates. Every single detail of your life." He gave me a rueful smile. "Between ourselves, I'm a theoretician, at heart. I want above all to understand the racial currents as they affect the ebb and flow of things here. What an admission! It's a weakness not always appreciated by my superiors who are more practical chaps. But there you are — we must live with our weaknesses. Time enough later to be saints, not so? I'd like to hear you try to explain yourself to me. But give me everything, mind. Don't stint yourself, and then I'll see if I can help you."

"But what in God's name is so special about me?"

"Given the way we are — our people in this country fall naturally, we believe, into separate groups. Not because they're forced to, mind you. Not at all. Though that's what the outside world believes. No, the fact is that they like it that way. They stick to their own. Same holds to same. Black to black, white to white, Asian to Asian, etcetera. But you, Harry — you're not like anyone. Who are you the same as? You don't belong to anything." His voice got really thick and throbbed in a very emotional way. "It's not that you're a stray, a common-or-garden outcast. No. You've made a whole damn career out of being different. I want to know why. And who is Harry Moto, exactly? A separate development, or parallel freedoms or equal opportunities, in the sense of groups — that we understand. But you — *you*, Harry, have made it a vocation! I must know what that means. Hell, man — " he came over and playfully punched me in the chest, gently, but with great ceremony, " — you've got so much to give us!" Then he wandered back to his desk and picked up his book. The interview was over. The front row of the scrum surrounded me again. As we got to the door, Dekker looked up. "And, remember, you can't take it with you. We can hold you for as long as we like. You do know that? I can hold you for rape, or immorality, or criminal association, assaulting a police officer — they talk of giving the poor old sarge a glass eye — I can hold you on any number of political grounds, I can hold you because I don't like the colour of your hair."

"I'll have to think."

"You do that, Harry. My men will help all they can." He peered at me "Moto . . . ? Moto . . . ? That's not a usual name. I knew a Moto, once. Bobby Moto I think it was. Played for Eastern Province. Flanker, I think. Very quick on a loose ball. You have any relations in Queenstown, Harry?"

In their eagerness to "help all they can" Dekker's men have been working on me with a vengeance. Lubavitch and Stokkies took to telling me bedtime stories about the dreadful effects of long-term solitary confinement, of demented prisoners who leaped from tenth-story windows, flung themselves down stairwells, strung themselves from their cell bars by their braces or contrived to slip on the soap in the shower and split their skulls like peas.

I think I know what Dekker wants from me. It isn't a "statement" in the usual sense at all but something that documents in the fullest possible way everything that I have been, everything I am. In short, a biography, a life. I have more or less decided to give it to him because it is my one chance of getting out of here. I'd feel a little happier if I didn't think my life meant more to him on paper than it does in the form to which I'm specially attached — i.e. the flesh. There was also the problem of how to give him what he wanted. The idea of sitting down and reciting it all for weeks was quite impossible. I knew I would have to find another way. It was on reflections like these that Dekker's men, working in shifts, rudely broke in, horribly eager "to help".

I think what finally decided me was the visit of ou Neels and Pielletjies who turned up in my cell with a grey canvas bag marked boldly in crisp black letters: STRICTLY PRIVATE. Pielletjies took from the bag a contraption that looked like a souped-up meat mincer with a turning handle, electronic gauges and trailing wires. Ou Neels ordered me on to my bunk. I put up a token resistance, skittering around my cell, my bare feet slapping the stone floor like a maniac butcher beating steak, and squealing helplessly. They threw me on the bunk and tied my hands while Stokkies pulled down my shorts and attached wires to my testicles with little clips that nipped like army ants. I went on screaming until Stokkies pulled a yellow duster out of the canvas bag and jammed it in my mouth and there I lay helpless, snivelling a bit, tied hand and foot and wired to this super mincer.

"Testing!" Pielletjies sang out, "nod your head when you feel something, Harry." And he began cranking the handle.

"Feel anything?" ou Neels peered anxiously into my face. I shook my head.

"Dammit!" cried Pielletjies turning the handle furiously until beads of sweat popped out on his forehead. "Check the galvanometer."

Ou Neels consulted the gauge. "Nothing. You're getting

piss-all current. Maybe the wires are crossed."

Pielletjies wiped the sweat out of his eyebrows and inspected the machine, peering into its innards and twitching the wires attached to my private parts so I screamed helplessly into the yellow duster. "It's probably bust. Or made in Korea, or something. You can depend on nothing these days. Come see here, Neels. It's all rusty inside, man."

"It rusts because they throw water on it sometimes to jack up the charge," ou Neels explained.

"Bladdy marvellous! How do they expect it to work properly if they let it rust just like this? "

"They told me in Stores," ou Neels said defensively, "they told me it had just been serviced."

"Oh well, we know all about Stores." Pielletjies began to untie me gloomily. "They'll tell you anything in Stores." He took the Bible and paged through it. "Sorry about this Harry. Didn't mean to mess you around. But perhaps it wasn't meant to be — this time. Perhaps we've seen God's hand in this."

"It was the rust," ou Neels muttered, unclipping the contact. He stopped and barked in my ear, "We're getting tired of you, kaffir. Time's running out."

Pielletjies found a bit he liked and smoothed back the pages with a huge palm. "Here, listen . . . 'Behold, to obey is better than sacrifice, and to harken than the fat of rams,' Samuel 15:22."

"He means that next time we'll fry your balls off." Ou Neels was angrily forcing the machine back into its canvas bag. He yanked the yellow duster out of my mouth. "Getting sick of waiting on you hand and foot."

It was the sight of Pielletjies riffling through the book that gave me the idea. I licked my lips and swallowed hard, my mouth dry and furry, and my dusty, pricking tongue feeling like carpet underlay. "There won't be a next time. I'd have told you if you'd given me a chance. I'm going to give you a statement."

The last time I saw Dekker he was reading *Cry, the Beloved Country* — and there wasn't a tear in sight.

"This is a great day. You've made the right decision. Congratulations. And you've done it of your own free will. Without pressure from us."

I couldn't believe my ears. "What do you mean — without pressure? Your people have hurt me."

"That's impossible. I would have heard. And I've heard nothing." His jaw set stubbornly and he looked out of the window.

"I'm just telling you what happened. Believe it or not. I must say it doesn't bode well for my statement if you're going to begin by calling me a liar."

He leaned back in his chair and thought this over. He shoved his little finger deep into his ear and jiggled it violently so it looked like a plump pink snake suddenly frightened and trying to squeeze into a hole too small for it. "I'm not calling you a liar. But you're making a serious charge. I'll tell you what, put it into writing and we'll investigate."

"That's what I plan to do."

"Come again?"

"I'll make the statement you want. But I'll do it in writing. This idea that I dictate it while somebody sits and writes it down, stopping me every two minutes with questions like — 'Puffdot . . . one "f" or two?' is not going to work. Let me put it down in my own way, in my own time."

Slowly he withdrew his pinky from its bolt-hole and examined it. It was thickly coated in ear-wax. He turned it in the light while considering my proposal, so that I saw the back of the finger with black hairs showing through the wax, a fat bee's leg yellow with pollen. Finally, he nodded gravely. "It could be a unique document. Life on the edge of our multi-ethnic society. A glimpse of the undeniable richness of our racial divisions. Living proof that oil and water won't mix . . . etcetera."

"Do you mean *apartheid?*"

"I mean ethnic independence of which there is no better example than Harry Moto — man apart."

"Listen, I'm just a guy with a funny skin and crinkled hair. I used to have breasts, too, once — and I've still got fallen arches. Don't build me up."

But he wasn't listening. He waved *Cry, the Beloved Country.* "You write it down, boy! It's going to be a picture of the soul of Africa. Like this!"

"I'm sorry, Mr Dekker, but to my mind, nothing so grand

exists. Africa! As far as I can see there is nothing but this place here and no one here but us — God help us."

He had made a little ball of the wax, rolling it between his thumb and forefinger, and he addressed his comments to it rather than to me. "I like a man with religious instincts."

"When do I start?" It was useless trying to explain. Dekker saw himself controlling the universe on the information I was going to give him.

"Soon as you like. Straight after your shower — if that suits?"

"What shower?"

"Relax, Harry. It's regulations, one, and two — don't want to be personal, but have you taken a whiff of yourself lately? If that's perfume you're wearing, it didn't come from Max Factor. Boy, you baff worse than a ricksha boy's armpit. Nothing personal. Besides, its only fitting. After years of hiding, you're coming clean." The tiny ball of wax glistened as he rolled it slowly, as if he held between his fingers the turning globe itself. The most terrible thing about Dekker was his sincerity: student, hygienist, philosopher — he really *did* want to understand, then to clean things up and finally to sort them out — for ever. Myself, most especially.

They have brought me paper in thick pads which smell of their blue bindings and a chicken's claw of blue ball-point pens tied in a rubber band. They have taken away my clothes — "for the disinfecting," ou Neels told me with a stagey sniff. I drape the towel around my shoulders and sit at the table, naked, in my cell. I examine the soap, butter yellow, oblong, second-hand, crossed with hairline cracks and preserving in its dried suds the last man's curled black hairs, stuck like fossils. I shall have to start writing. It's silly to feel exposed. When I've finished I'll be free. Or in Dekker's words, "You shan't need to continue, as it were, in this place . . . " He asked if I saw what he meant. I see what he means. And it frightens me. For the moment attention has shifted from Harry in the flesh to Harry on the paper. That will be the case for as long as I go on writing. As long as I have a story to tell, life goes on. I am the beginning and the ending.

Very well then, begin . . .